CIVILIAN CAPACITY BUILDING FOR PEACE OPERATIONS IN A CHANGING WORLD ORDER

AN INDIAN PERSPECTIVE

CIVILIAN CAPACITY BUILDING FOR PEACE OPERATIONS IN A CHANGING WORLD ORDER

An Indian Perspective

Editors

PK Singh

V K Saxena

Sandeep Dewan

(Established 1870)

United Service Institution of India

New Delhi

Vij Books India Pvt Ltd

New Delhi (India)

Published by

Vij Books India Pvt Ltd
(Publishers, Distributors & Importers)
2/19, Ansari Road
Delhi – 110 002
Phones: 91-11-43596460, 91-11-47340674
Fax: 91-11-47340674
e-mail: vijbooks@rediffmail.com

Copyright © 2013, United Service Institution of India, New Delhi

ISBN: 978-93-82652-24-3

Contents

CHAPTER 1

INTRODUCTION

CIVILIAN CAPACITY FOR PEACE OPERATIONS

IN A CHANGING WORLD ORDER

General

United Nations (UN) peacekeeping has for last six decades been a flagship enterprise of the UN. The people in conflict affected countries think that 'Blue Helmets' are the UN. They have a valid expectation that with the arrival of the Blue Helmets, violence, deprivation and despair will no longer rule their lives. They hope that the 'Peace keepers' will provide them safety, security, food, shelter and medicine. The 'Blue Helmets' have always lived up to the expectations of the people they set out to serve. The report of the UN panel on review of peacekeeping operations, under chairmanship of Lakhdar Brahimi, is clear that peace operations entail three principal activities: conflict prevention and peacemaking; peacekeeping and peace building. Conflict prevention and peacemaking address the potential for conflict with the purpose of trying to prevent eruption of conflict. Despite such efforts, should conflict break out, peacemaking attempts to bring it to halt, using the tools of diplomacy and mediation. Peacekeeping as a six decades old enterprise had evolved rapidly from a traditional primarily military model of observing cease-fires and force separation after inter-state wars, to incorporate a complex model of many elements, military and civilian, working together to maintain peace in the dangerous aftermath of violent conflict. Peace-building is a term of relatively more recent origin and defines activities undertaken on far side of conflict to reassemble the foundations of peace and provide the tools for building on those foundations something that is more than absence of war. Thus it includes, but not limited to reintegrating former combatants into civil society, strengthening the rule of law, improving respect for human rights through the monitoring, education and investigation of past and existing abuses; providing technical assistance for democratic development; and promoting conflict resolution and reconciliation techniques. Peace Building is to provide basic security, deliver peace dividends, build confidence in political process, strengthen capacity to lead peace building and lay the foundation for sustained development. The peace building sometimes steps into realm of state building or nation building which is beyond the charter of the UN.[1]

The process of peace building starts with the deployment of 'Peace Keepers' in a conflict affected country. Peace keeping operations mandated by the Security Council have been the main instrument for UN action on ground for conflict resolution. They have stood the test of time and will remain the critical pillar of UN activities for years to come. With many of the situations where UN peacekeeping missions are operating being those of prolonged conflict or post conflict, it is essential that the UN peacekeeping missions involve themselves in building local capacities for provision of basic administration and essential services. Civilian capacities are critical in this endeavour and their presence in a significantly enhanced manner in peacekeeping missions must be ensured ab initio.

Over the years, peacekeeping has become multidirectional and the mandates have expanded to include protection of civilians, confidence building measures, electoral process, rule of law, and economic and social developments. It is, therefore, important that the key requirements of peacekeeping are adequately resourced and its structures strengthened. At the same time the post conflict situations and, indeed, those of prolonged conflict demand that serious attention is paid to building basic government structures and

---

1   For the Honour of India, A History of Indian Peacekeeping, Lieutenant General Satish Nambiar, PVSM, AVSM, VrC (Retd), Centre for Armed Forces Historical Research, United Service Institute of India, 2009.

providing basic services, without which the chances of lapsing into conflict multiply manifold. Civilian capacities, including correctional services, legal and other services which form core government functions, are very important for ensuring basic administration and need to be incorporated into the UN ambit.[2]

India's experience in transforming a colonial legacy into a modern, dynamic nation that is both a democracy and a rapidly growing economy made Indian peacekeepers instinctively understand that no peace can be effective unless it is accompanied by growth of local institutions. Indian peacekeepers in various UN missions have made conscious efforts to assist local authorities in restoring national structures that had collapsed during conflict. They donned peace building hats and helped restore administrative processes, strengthened local policing and activated judicial mechanisms in areas they have served. They worked through indigenous mechanisms for conflict resolution and mediation in order to strengthen these local institutions so that they become viable political institutions. They also tried to get educational institutions to function and provided services such as livestock clinics to help local economies get going. Details are at Annexure 1.

India stands solidly committed to assist the UN in the maintenance of international peace and security. It has a proud history of UN peacekeeping dating back to its inception in the 1950s. India has participated in some of the world's most difficult peacekeeping missions and over 155,000 Indian troops have donned the Blue Beret in 43 of the 61 UN missions conducted so far. Today India is the third largest troop contributor with 8,109 personnel deployed with nine UN Peacekeeping Missions of which 1,039 are police personnel, including the first Female Formed Police Unit under the UN. Besides contingent troops, formed police units and individual police personnel, India has provided 72 experts to various current UN peacekeeping missions. In the whole UN system, except field missions by DPKO and DPA, there are about 1897 Indian

---

2 Statement by Ambassador Manjeev Singh Puri, Deputy Permanent Representative of India at the United Nations, in the General Assembly Debate on SAG's Report to SG on Civilian Capacity Review on 11 May 2011.

professionals (P and GS staff). In addition there are about 2400 Field Staff in various organisations of the UN. The Indian troops, police personnel and civilians deployed on UN Missions have maintained high standards of performance under challenging circumstances. They have voluntarily undertaken the peace building activities to win over hearts and minds of local people.

India has been included as one of the countries where capacity in several areas has been noted for possible tapping by the UN. In the past when called upon to provide civilian capacities for UN missions, India has responded in a prompt manner. It has provided several officials on secondment basis to the UN missions in former Yugoslavia and right now in Afghanistan.[3] But the UN only makes use of secondment system for peacemaking operations in exceptional circumstances when specialists are needed which cannot be recruited through the normal recruitment channel.

India's unique combination of being the largest democracy in the world with a strong tradition of respect for rule of law and the successful experience in nation building makes it particularly relevant in the context of twenty-first century peace building. India was reappointed to the Organisational Committee of the Peace Building Commission (PBC) in December 2010, for a third two year term. India is strongly supportive of nationally-led plans for peace consolidation.

It is critical that civilian capacity deployments are demand driven. Capacity mapping to locate existing capacities appears a useful tool, however, peace cannot be restored to post-conflict societies and their citizens cannot be freed from fear and want unless national authorities are able to govern effectively. The capacity of effective governance, in turn, depends on the existence of institutions that enable these authorities to respond effectively to the aspirations of people. This general political aphorism is substantiated by the experience of the international community

---

3 Statement by Ambassador Manjeev Singh Puri, Deputy Permanent Representative of India at the United Nations, in the Security Council Debate on SAG's Report to SG on Civilian Capacity Review on 12 May 2011.

in its peacekeeping and peace building efforts during the last two decades. It is pertinent to mention that peacekeeping and peace building activities are inseparably inter-linked. They run in tandem and concurrently. Peacekeepers are the path finder and pioneer of the Peace Building process.

India's Perspective on UN Operations

Over the years, India's response and unreserved participation in UN peacekeeping operations has been both spontaneous and enthusiastic. Given that independent India has been beset by more than its fair share of domestic problems, its contribution to the maintenance of international peace and security has been quite remarkable. As one of the founding member of the United Nations, during the Cold War period, India was in the forefront of the efforts to promote causes important to the developing world, of which she herself was a substantial part. It pursued an active international policy of independence, lasting peace, social justice, freedom, social progress and economic development especially in the developing countries of Asia and Africa. In the post-Cold War world, India's policy has been directed at moderating the unilateralism of the more powerful countries of the developed world.

India's policy is to follow the force generation model of the DPKO to generate civilian capacities also. The method for generating military capacity for the DPKO is known as 'DPKO Force Generation Model'. The process involves generation, rotation, and repatriation for the formed units and individuals. The process starts with planning by Military Planning Service (MPS). This planning results in concept of operation and Force Requirement (FR). The FR includes the mission, tasks, organization and number of personnel required. The mission receives its mandate from the Security Council Resolution (SCR). However, the planning often commences well before the SCR. A Technical Assessment Mission (TAM) goes to the mission area and decides on the mission factors and Troop Cost reimbursements. The Force Generation Team interacts with Troops Contributing Country and finalizes MOU and a FR is drafted for each unit in accordance with the concept of operations. After following internal bureaucratic process the TCC confirms availability of the required resources and units/individuals are deployed.

The force generation model of the DPKO is normally followed by the Government of India for providing civilian capacity to the United Nations or to the friendly countries on bilateral basis. Request for providing civilian capacity is first received by the Ministry of External Affairs. The ministry considers the desirability of providing the requested civilian capacity keeping various political and diplomatic considerations in mind. The request, if found worthy of acceptance, is forwarded to the concerned ministry for feasibility evaluation. The ministry, in turn, asks its departments to assess the availability of suitable personnel willing to proceed to the concerned destination. In case the concerned ministry does not find enough resource from its departments, it may outsource the requirement from affiliated Non-government Organisations.

The details of availability/non-availability are forwarded to the Ministry of External Affairs where necessary political clearance is given. The Government of India prefers to provide civilian capacity out of the existing Government employees on secondment basis. The members of the civil society may apply directly to the UN for the advertised vacancies. Since the requests for providing civilian capacity have been so few and far in between that the need for establishing rosters or capacity matching system has not been felt. It is pertinent to mention that the Government of India responds positively to the request for providing civilian capacity subject to desirability and availability of the required capacity within the Government resources. India's view as articulated by the acting Permanent Representative of India is that the recruitment model adopted for generating civilian capacity should give primacy to a partnership with the Governments of Member States.

This procedure has the following inbuilt advantages:-

(a) It gives the United Nations rapid access to the required capacities.

(b) It allows rapid scaling up and scaling down of capacities.

(c) It provides capacities trained to work in an established Government structures.

(d) It would mesh well with the peacekeeping personnel on the ground.

With constantly expanding mandates, it is imperative that adequate resources are placed at the disposal of peacekeeping missions. The missions must involve themselves in building local capacities for provision of basic administration and essential services and start meaningful peace building process and activities.

India supports nationally led plans for peace consolidation process. National actors and institutions of the affected countries should provide the primary source of civilian capacity. International capacity should provide mechanism of last resort.

India respects the ownership of the affected countries and provides peace building and state building support to the affected countries when required and where required as development partnership on bilateral or multi-lateral basis and through the United Nations. India is of the view that the civilian capacity should be enhanced to improve the capabilities of the peacekeeping missions. They should not be allowed to dilute or detract the requirement of peacekeeping. The peacekeepers are compulsive peace builders and the peace building and peacekeeping activities are inseparably inter-linked. The Blue Helmets must act as hub centre of all peace building activities. They provide the umbrella for peace building. The unity of command must be maintained to ensure that the peace building does not fall victim of turf battle between peacekeepers and peace builders.

CHAPTER 2

CIVILIAN CAPACITY BUILDING – THE INDIAN WAY

The UN Dilemma

The UN finds it difficult to identify candidates in certain specialized categories, including in security sector reform, judicial and prisons management.[4] This is partly due to the non-availability of these skills in the marketplace in general. India has a vast reservoir of experienced civilian capacity in the Government, semi-government, non-government and corporate sectors. The capacity in government and semi-government sectors is well organised and time tested systems are in place to ensure speedy and appropriate response to requests for civilian capacity from the United Nations as well as bilateral requests from friendly countries. However, the civilian capacity in non-government and corporate sector are not so well coordinated and harnessed. The tasks of civilian experts in UN Peace Missions usually ranges across a multitude of activities mainly focused on state building, eg capacity development in the justice sector, governance and public administration, institution building, safety and Security, economic revitalisation and reintegration. The civilian experts for these activities are available in India. The details are discussed in the succeeding paragraphs.

The Indian Technical and Economic Cooperation

Since the civilian component of any UN operation would necessarily be a common part of today's multidimensional missions, creating a rostered civilian capacity is being pursued by several national, regional and international actors worldwide.[5] Over the years,

---

4 Cedric de Conning, Addressing the Civilian Peace Keeping Capacity Gap, Conflict Trends.

5 Government of India, Ministry of External affairs, Technical Cooperation Division available on http://www.itec.mea.gov.in.

while the demand for qualified and specialised civilian personnel has increased, more and more human resource organisations have become involved in UN operations, which has necessitated the rostering approach by governments as well as international organisations. As a result, rostering experts into pools and databases have become a mainstream, standard approach in want of a better solution.

As part of the post conflict nation building process, the most important task before the affected countries is the promotion of social and economic advancement of their people which had been retarded and in most cases reversed during the years of conflict or unrest. Skilled manpower and experts, financial resources, infrastructure packages and build-up of technology are the bottlenecks to be overcome. To meet the challenges of socio-economic development, cooperative efforts of the developing countries are as important as assistance from developed countries and international organisations. India has made substantial progress and gained useful experience in industrial and technological development after it regained its freedom in 1947.

The Indian Technical and Economic Cooperation (ITEC) Programme of the Ministry of External Affairs is an earnest attempt by India to share the fruits of its socio-economic development and technological achievement with other developing countries. The programme was launched on 15 September 1964 as a bilateral programme of assistance of the Government of India. It is the flagship programme of the Indian Government's technical cooperation effort, not only because of its wide geographical coverage but also for innovative forms of technical cooperation. Being essentially bilateral in nature, ITEC is about cooperation and partnership for mutual benefit. It is demand-driven and response-oriented. It is focused on addressing the needs of developing countries.

The ITEC Programme, fully-funded by the Government of India, has evolved and grown over the years. Under ITEC and its corollary SCAAP (Special Commonwealth African Assistance Programme), 158 countries in Asia, East Europe, Central Asia, Africa, Latin

America, the Caribbean as well as Pacific and Small Island countries are invited to share the Indian developmental experience in various fields. As a result of various activities under the ITEC programme, there is now a visible and growing awareness among other countries about the competence of India as a provider of technical know-how and expertise as well as training opportunities, consultancy services and feasibility studies. This assistance programme has generated immense goodwill and substantive cooperation among developing countries.

The ITEC Programme constitutes an integral part of India's South-South Cooperation effort which has been a traditional pillar of the country's foreign policy and diplomacy. The ITEC Programme has six components, which are as follows:-

(a) Training (civilian and defence) in India of nominees from ITEC partner countries.

(b) Projects and project related activities such as feasibility studies and consultancy services.

(c) Deputation of Indian experts abroad.

(d) Study tours.

(e) Gifting/Donation of equipment.

(f) Aid for Disaster Relief.

The training programmes have contributed to capacity building and human resource development in many parts of the world. The ITEC/SCAAP programme is a visible symbol of India's role and contribution to South-South Cooperation. While the ITEC Programme has been envisaged essentially as a bilateral programme, there have been instances when ITEC resources have been used for financing technical cooperation programmes conceived in regional and inter-regional context such as Economic Commission for Africa, Industrial Development Unit of Commonwealth Secretariat, UNIDO, Group of 77 and G-15. In more recent years, its activities have also been associated with regional and multilateral organizations and cooperation groupings like Association of South East Asian Nations (ASEAN), Bay of Bengal Initiative for Multi-Sectorial Technical and Economic Cooperation (BIMSTEC), Mekong-Ganga Cooperation (MGC), African Union (AU), Afro-Asian Rural Development Organization (AARDO), Pan African Parliament, Caribbean Community (CARICOM), World Trade Organization (WTO) and Indian Ocean Rim – Association for Regional Cooperation (IOR–ARC). A brief of the civilian capacity provided by India under the ITEC programme to 75 countries is placed at Annexure 2.

Training

Training or capacity building is one of the major activities under ITEC. Professionals and people from developing countries are offered unique training courses, both civilian and defence, in different centres of excellence in India which empower them with not just professional skills, but prepare them for an increasingly globalised world.

(a) **Civilian Training Programme**. It is fully sponsored by the Government of India. 42 institutions conduct around 200 short-term, medium-term and long-term courses every year. The training programme is demand-driven and subjects selected are of interest to developing countries for their working professionals on a wide and diverse range of skills and disciplines. The courses have been divided into seven broad categories for easy identification - Government Courses, IT and Telecommunication, Management, Rural Development, Specialised Courses, Technical Courses, Environment and Renewable Energy Courses. The most sought after courses are in the field of Information Technology and Linguistics (English). Training is imparted to Government officials in areas such as Finance & Accounts, Audit, Banking, Education Planning & Administration, Parliamentary Studies, Crime Records, Management, Environment, etc. Every year, around 5000 slots are allocated to ITEC partner countries to attend various civilian training courses in India. An encouraging trend of senior level participants from within and outside

Government joining ITEC courses has been noticed – a clear affirmation that ITEC courses have come to be recognised as useful tools for capacity building, empowerment and upgrading of skills.

(b) **Defence Training**. This covers training to personnel belonging to all the three wings of Defence Services, viz. Army, Air Force & Navy, nominated by the ITEC partner countries in prestigious institutions like National Defence College, Defence Services Staff College, etc. The facility is also extended and availed by some select developed countries. The training field covers Security and Strategic Studies, Defence Management, Marine and Aeronautical Engineering, Logistics and Management, etc.

Project-Related Cooperation

India assists ITEC partner countries, on the basis of mutually agreed projects, to establish useful infrastructure facilities with technology and skills appropriate to their resources and needs. Through project assistance, India also demonstrates the skills, technologies and human resource capabilities, which it has acquired in the course of its own development. A number of bilateral projects are undertaken, notably in the fields of Archaeological Conservation, Information Technology (IT) and Small and Medium Enterprises (SMEs). Feasibility studies and consultancy services, at the request of ITEC partner countries, are carried out under the Programme. Results of these studies are handed over to the Governments concerned.

Deputation of Indian Experts

Indian experts are deputed to friendly countries on their request to assist in developmental activities. Some of the fields covered are Creative Arts, Pest Management, Military training, IT, Audit, various disciplines of Medicine, English teaching, Telecommunications, Agricultural research etc. Indian experiences and expertise in the fields of small and medium scale industries, agriculture and financial management are particularly relevant to the developing countries.

Study Tours

Study tours in India are undertaken at the specific request of ITEC partner countries. Specific areas of interest are identified and a two to three weeks programme is arranged during which the delegates are taken to important institutions, training centres, etc. in different parts of India.

Gifts/Donation of Equipment

The Government of India, under the ITEC Programme, provides gifts/donations of equipment to ITEC partner countries to assist in their developmental efforts. These gifts/donations are usually in response to requests of these friendly countries and the commitments made by Prime Minister, External Affairs Minister etc.

Aid for Disaster Relief

Under this Programme, India supplies humanitarian aid like food grains, medicines, woollen blankets and similar other items to countries struck by natural disasters.

Requisition of Experts and Civilian Capacities

The Technical Cooperation Division of the Ministry of External affairs, Government of India provides deputation of experts and civilian capacities under the ITEC programme. The application form for requisitioning such capacity is at Annexure 3. The application form for undergoing courses fully funded by the Ministry of External affairs, Government of India is at Annexure 4.

CHAPTER 3

INDIAN CIVILIAN CAPACITY PROVIDERS

Development Partnership Agency

India has recently set up its own international aid agency similar to USAID and UK's Department for International Development (DFID), with an estimated corpus of a sizable $ 15 billion to be spent over the next five years. This new agency, called Development Partnership Administration (DPA), will oversee all the development partnership projects that India will undertake in developing countries around the world.[6] The DPA is headed by an Additional Secretary of the Ministry of External Affairs' (MEA) and will bring under one umbrella all agencies involved with foreign aid and development projects within the MEA. The DPA is being formed by streamlining three different organisations within the MEA that currently oversee India-sponsored development projects abroad.

In the words of Mr Syed Akbaruddin, joint secretary with the Ministry of External Affairs, "We (India) do not like to call ourselves a donor", "We call it development partnership because it is in the framework of sharing development experiences. It follows a model different from that followed in the conventional North-South economic cooperation patterns, hence the designation of Development Partnership Administration, it is administering our development partnership projects."

Under the grants assistance scheme, India has made significant contributions in many countries, specifically in the South Asia region in the areas of education, IT, energy and healthcare. Efforts such as post-war reconstruction projects in Sri Lanka, hydroelectric power projects with Bhutan, which is the biggest recipient of Indian aid (Rs

---

6 Ibid.

1,330 crore in 2010-11), road connectivity projects with Myanmar, which will connect the India's Mizoram with the Myanmar port of Sittwe and recently a multitude of development projects in Afghanistan including recent plans to export more than 1.5 lakh tonnes of wheat to the struggling nation are some instances of India's growing influence via foreign development projects.

About ten years ago, Indian foreign aid projects were very limited both in terms of resources and geographical spread. However, today the reach of Indian aid has spread around the world with more than 60 countries benefiting from India sponsored projects. IT projects in many African nations have been a thrust area. DPA is an agency meant to streamline implementation, not to lay down policy. India's foreign projects under the DPA will work around strict considerations of mutual benefits. Many projects do have spin-offs of promotions of Indian exports and India's requirements to access all important international energy resources. For example, India's energy projects in Sudan and South Sudan have also provided opportunity for Indian companies to contribute to local communities via many social projects, including the recent distribution of thousands of footballs to schools and children's camps due to the popularity of the sport in the African continent.

Election Commission of India

India is a socialist, democratic republic and the largest democracy in the world. The constitution of India has vested in the Election Commission of India (EC) the superintendence, direction, and control of the entire process for conduct of elections to Parliament, legislature of every state and the office of President and Vice President of India.[7]

International Cooperation

(a)   India is a founding member of the International Institute of Democracy and Electoral Assistance (IDEA),

---

7 Election Commission of India available at http://eci.nic.in.

Stockholm, Sweden. In the recent past, the Commission has expanded international contacts by way of sharing experience and expertise in the areas of Electoral Management and Administration, Electoral laws and Reforms. Election officials from the national electoral bodies and other delegates from several countries like Russia, Sri Lanka, Nepal, Indonesia, South Africa, Bangladesh, Thailand, Nigeria, Namibia, Bhutan, Australia, the United States and Afghanistan etc have visited the Commission for better understanding of Indian electoral process. The Commission has also provided experts and observers for elections to other countries in cooperation with the United Nations and Common Wealth Secretariat.[8]

(b)   India is the Vice Chairperson of the Association of Asian Election Authorities (AAEA). The ECI is supporting Common Wealth Nations, specially the developing and African countries in improving Election Management and Democratic practices. A batch of senior officials from Afghanistan has received training in India and Jordan has requested ECI for assistance in election management and electoral reforms.

(c)   The Election Commission of India has signed a Memorandum of Understanding with the Washington based International Foundation for Electoral Systems for developing and strengthening democratic institutions and processes. The focus of the MOU is making available the knowledge and experience of ESI to election managers and practitioners around the world through India International Institute of Democracy and Election Management.

(d)   Heads of Election Commissions of SAARC countries have signed and adopted a charter to promote mutual contact and learning for enhancing their capabilities towards conducting free and fair elections.

---

8   ECI Press Notes ECI/PN/13/2011, ECI/PN/39/2011, ECI/PN/58/2011, ECI/PN/25/2012, ECI/PN/40/2012 and ECI/PN/43/2012.

Memorandum of Understanding. The EC has signed a Memorandum of Understanding with the United Nations for cooperation in electoral matters. The parties have agreed to promote cooperation, on mutually agreed terms and conditions in priority areas in the field of electoral assistance. Besides the MOU with the United Nations, the EC has also signed bilateral MoU with Ivory Coast, United Mexican State, Bhutan, Afghanistan, Brazil, Russia, Nepal, Chile, Indonesia and South Africa. The text of the MoU is at Annexure 5.

National Disaster Management Authority

On 23 December 2005, the Government of India enacted the Disaster Management Act, which envisaged the creation of the National Disaster Management Authority (NDMA), headed by the Prime Minister, and State Disaster Management Authorities (SDMAs) headed by respective Chief Ministers, to spearhead and implement a holistic and integrated approach to Disaster Management in India. NDMA as the apex body is mandated to lay down the policies, plans and guidelines for Disaster Management to ensure timely and effective response to disasters.

The National Disaster Relief Force (NDRF) consists of 10 battalions which will soon be increased to 12 battalions. These units are located at various strategic locations throughout India. There are about 180 Search and Rescue Teams fully trained and equipped for any emergency. Out of these about 14 teams are kept ready on wheels for deployment within 30 minutes of any emergency.[9]

International Assistance. On 11 March 2011 a massive earthquake struck Japan's Tohoku region resulting in a Tsunami and radioactive leakage from the Fukushima nuclear power plant. Subsequently, one team of NDRF consisting of 46 personnel equipped with latest Search & Rescue and CBRN equipment was deployed in the affected area to assist the local authorities in relief and rehabilitation efforts under tough and trying conditions.. The team working in sub-zero temperature recovered 7 dead bodies and Japanese currency worth

---

9   National Disaster Management Authority, Government of India available at http://ndma.gov.in.

fifty million yen. NDRF's contribution was widely appreciated by the Japanese Government, people and media.

Professional USAR Support During Disasters Which Result in Structural Collapse. The UNGA Resolution 57/150 of 16 December 2002 on "Strengthening the Effectiveness and Coordination of International USAR Assistance" endorses the International Search and Rescue Advisory Group (INSARAG) Guidelines as the principal reference for the coordination of international USAR response. The INSARAG Guidelines, developed and practiced by emergency responders from around the world, serve to guide international USAR teams and disaster-affected countries during international USAR response operations. In an effort to achieve this objective, the INSARAG community has developed a voluntary, independent, peer review process, the INSARAG External Classification (IEC). The IEC has been unanimously endorsed by the INSARAG Steering Group (ISG). To ensure that a USAR team's international response capability remains current and continues to subscribe to the INSARAG methodology, the ISG has also endorsed the INSARAG External Reclassification (IER) process. Taken together these two processes form the INSARAG Classification System.

The India's capacity is yet to be classified under IEC. However, the INSARAG focuses on structural collapse only whereas NDMF of India manages all kinds of disasters including nuclear disaster.

National Institute of Disaster Management

The National Institute of Disaster Management (NIDM) was constituted under an Act of Parliament with a vision to play the role of premier institute for capacity development in India and the region. The Institute supports six Centres of Excellence in the areas of flood risk management, earthquake risk management, cyclone risk management, drought risk management, landslide risk management and management of industrial disaster.

NIDM hosts the SAARC Disaster Management Centre (SDMC)

and works as its national focal point. NIDM, New Delhi, India has been conferred the title of " World Centre of Excellence on Landslide Risk Reduction" by the International Consortium on Landslides (ICL) and Global Promotion Committee (GPC) of the International Programme on Landslides under International Strategy for Disaster Reduction (IPL-ISDR) during the second World Landslide Forum held at FAQ Headquarters, Rome, Italy between 3-7 October 2011.[10]

---

10 National Institute of Disaster Management, Ministry of Home Affairs, Government of India available at http://nidm.gov.in.

CHAPTER 4

CIVILIAN CAPACITY RESOURCE POTENTIAL IN INDIA

Safety and Security

The activities related to community violence reduction, disarmament, demobilisation and weapon management should be entrusted to the serving as well as retired army, police and paramilitary forces officers. Services of serving officers could be requisitioned through the Government channels and retired officers could be through Government/semi-government and non-government channels. The numbers of experts available for these activities are far more than the anticipated requirement. Keeping in view the sensitivities of these activities it is advisable to follow the DPKO force generation model for these activities.

Reform of Police and other Law Enforcement Agencies

The activities like armed violence reduction, human resource management, sexual and gender based violence, criminal investigation, public order, community policing, traffic management and small arms control should be left to local police of the concerned state in accordance with the principle of 'ownership'. However, capacity of the local police should be built by giving them training and consultancy. Some senior retired police officers would be available and willing to serve on a peace mission of this nature. The Government of India could be approached by the concerned State to send an Indian Police Training Team (IPTRAT).

Protection of Civilians

Protection of civilians has a very wide spectrum. It includes Physical Security, Protection of Women and Children, Health, Water &

Sanitation, Hunger, Hygiene & Habitat, Basic Infrastructure, Rehabilitation of Social Sector and Psychological Protection. These activities must be performed by the concerned Government according to the principles of 'ownership' and 'partnership'. The supporting countries, UN Mission, Agencies and Funds must act as facilitators only. The expertise in the non-government sector should be rostered and utilised on as required basis. Resources available with the State Governments in India could be utilised on either bilateral basis or through the UN as most of these activities are state subjects in India.

Rule of Law

The word 'peacekeeping' has been employed to include a large number of military and related activities involving the use of force in self-defence or the immediate defence of non-combatants, for observing ceasefire and force separation to bring peace in conflict ridden state(s). The key objective of peacekeeping has been to help preserve the international state system. The post-conflict peace-building (PCPB) measures initiated by the United Nations (UN) and some of its Member-States in conflict-ridden societies have been unsuccessful in the recent past. With the dominance of military personnel, the approach has remained confined to demobilization, disarmament and re-integration of former combatants. In fact, the potential of the UN to adopt an integrated approach to peace-building has not been fully developed, by either the UN or its agencies and the deployment of civilians in international peace operations has remained a marginal issue. The Brahimi Report (2000) brought out certain shortcomings in the peacekeeping system. This has resulted in a qualitative transformation in peacekeeping efforts, and the proportion of civilians in multi-dimensional missions is increasing. For instance, as on 28 February 2013, nearly 5100 international civilians were serving in peacekeeping operations worldwide. However, one of the persistent criticisms levelled against the existing system is that a group of developed states has been 'ganging-up' for top positions, with the domestic actors being forced to make do with positions pre-agreed among the external actors. Such an approach does not encourage local ownership and the contextualization of responses to the local needs, priorities and socio-cultural environment, and thus leads to failure of the PCPB missions. A paper on the Indian perspective of the Rule of Law is placed at Annexure 6.

Reintegration

The integration process entails empowering individuals and enables them to find life sustaining employment/occupation to start a new life. Development of technical skills can help them in meaningful reintegration with society. India has a wide network of about one thousand Industrial Training Institutes (ITIs) and their self-financing counterparts i.e. Industrial Training Centres (ITCs). These training Institutes and Centres provide training in engineering and non-engineering technical fields. The main objective behind opening of ITIs is to provide technical manpower to the fast emerging secondary sector i.e. industrial sector of the developing and developed economies. There are both Government funded and private (self-financing) ITIs in India. Most ITIs impart training in a couple of hundred technical trades like fitter, plumber, mechanic, electrician, etc. The Government India can be approached either to open ITIs in the target country or required number of vacancies can be allotted in the ITIs in India. Similarly, Industrial Training Centres could be approached to open a training facility in the target country or make some seats available for training in India.

Security Sector Reforms

Defence Sector Reforms, Transnational Organised Crime and Trafficking, Counter Terrorism, Border Management and Immigration are best left to the professional Army, Police and BSF officers. The serving officers can be employed on secondment basis and retired officers can be hired through rosters and placement agencies. Adequate numbers of such officers are available in India.

Prison and Correction Reforms

The issues like Policy, Planning and Institutional Reforms in prisons,

Health in Prisons, Mental Health in Prison, Gender in Prisons, Juvenile Detention, Prisoner Education and Vocational Training, Prison Registries, probation and Parole are the issues which must be left to the experts in Prison Management. Such experts will be difficult to find in the civil street. The required number of experts can be hired through the Government of India. Some of the senior retired police officers with the experience of serving in prisons can be employed through normal recruitment system of the UN or on contractual basis.

Judicial and Legal System Reform

Judicial and legal system reforms have a very wide spectrum spreading over policy, planning and institutional reforms, law reform and legislative drafting, constitution making, legislative oversight and legal revision, sentencing policy, accountability and oversight of judicial institutions, legal training and professional education, judiciary, investigation and prosecution, child protection and juvenile justice, criminal law and procedures, civil and administrative law and procedures, informal justice, Sharia/Islamic law, military justice etc. The Bar Council of India is a statutory body created by Parliament to regulate and represent the Indian bar. It performs the regulatory function by prescribing standards of professional conduct and etiquette and by exercising disciplinary jurisdiction over the bar. The council performs certain representative functions by protecting the rights, privileges and interests. It also organizes welfare schemes for them. The Bar Council of India could be source of finding legal experts.[11] The All India Bar Association maintains a directory of lawyers and Law Firms. The association works in close coordination with non-governmental organizations, government and non-statutory bodies and international organisations. The All India Bar Association can be good source of identifying legal experts. The requirement of judicial officers and senior judges should be met out of the serving personnel through the Ministry of External Affairs and Ministry of Law and Justice.[12] India has a vast reservoir

---

11 Bar Council of India available at http://www.barcouncilofindia.org.

12 All India Bar Association available at http://www.allindiabar.org.

of legal and constitutional experts both in Government and non-government sectors. In the Government sector Ministry of Law and Justice is the nodal ministry. However, all requests for secondment should be routed through the Ministry of External Affairs.

Economic Revitalisation

Economic revitalisation is achieved through 'employment generation' and 'Local Economic Recovery'. Employment generation may include cash for work schemes, skill training, in-camp economies for IDPs etc. Local economic recovery could entail vocational training, micro financing, small and medium size enterprises, creation of green jobs, etc. Towards economic upliftment of its rural masses, the Government of India has launched a massive Cash for Work Scheme called the Mahatma Gandhi National Rural Employment Guarantee Act (MGNREGA).

Mahatma Gandhi National Rural Employment Guarantee Act

The Mahatma Gandhi National Rural Employment Guarantee Act (MGNREGA) is an Indian job guarantee scheme, enacted by legislation on 25 August 2005. The scheme provides a legal guarantee for one hundred days of employment in every financial year to adult members of any rural household willing to do public work-related unskilled manual work at the statutory minimum wage of Rs 120 ($ 2.17) per day in 2009 prices The Central government outlay for scheme is Rs 40,000 crore ($ 7.24 billion) in FY 2010–11. This act was introduced with an aim of improving the purchasing power of the rural people, primarily semi or un-skilled workers living in rural India, whether or not they are below the poverty line. Around one-third of the stipulated work force is women. The act directs state governments to implement MGNREGA "schemes". Under the MGNREGA the Central Government meets the cost towards the payment of wage, 3/4 of material cost and some percentage of administrative cost. State Governments meet the cost of unemployment allowance, 1/4 of material cost and administrative cost of State council. Since the State Governments pay the unemployment allowance, they are heavily incentivised to offer employment to workers. The expertise gained in these areas can be gainfully utilised to promote economic recovery and to generate employment.

Core Government Functionality

Areas like aid effectiveness, fiscal accountability, parliamentary strengthening and support, local governance, public administration reforms, public financial management, risk management, core cabinet and executive process and anti-corruption can be addressed effectively by drawing upon huge resources in Government and non-government sectors.

Consultancy Development Centre

The Consultancy Development Centre (CDC) came into being as a registered society in January 1986, and is functioning from its office at India Habitat Centre Complex, New Delhi. It is an autonomous institution of Department of Scientific and Industrial Research (DSIR). In order to enhance technological and managerial capabilities of consultants and export capabilities of consultants, the Centre has developed interactions with international organizations such as World Bank, Asian Development Bank, ESCAP and APCTT. The Centre has arranged programmes for consultants at national and international levels. CDC has been identified to be a nodal agency for Technical Consultancy Development Programmes for Asia and Pacific (TCDPAP). CDC maintains a database of Consultants and Consultancy Organisations. There profiles are upgraded on regular basis. The Centre is a functional roster of Consultants and experts in almost every field.[13]

Ecological Warriors

India is fast developing in industrial, social and technological spheres. There are large infrastructural requirements to meet the growing needs. Due to sudden acceleration in growth of industry;

---

13 Consultancy Development Centre, Government of India available at www.cdc.org.in.

pressure on agriculture land, water resources and forests is unprecedented. The ill effects of this enormous growth in terms of ecological degradation were foreseen and vividly read by Dr Norman Borlaugh who suggested to the then Prime Minister, Mrs Indira Gandhi to address this menace on a war footing by involving the Army. Mrs Indira Gandhi and Mr M Swaminathan understood the gravity of situation and cleared the proposal of raising Ecological Battalions in the Country by involving army. This resulted in raising of first Ecological Battalion at Dehradun with the primary aim of greening and rehabilitating over-mined Mussorie hills. The Ecological Battalions of TA are one of its kinds in the world. These battalions are also commonly called as Ecological Task Forces (ETF). The responsibility of greening India has been entrusted to these battalions who take up projects for various States and complete them in a time bound manner. The enrolment in ETFs is based on Ex-servicemen of respective States who after going on discharge from active service are still physically fit to undertake afforestation and other ecological tasks. Further details of Ecological Warriors are placed at Annexure 7.

Innovation and Invention

Descriptions of innovation in India which originate in the frugal innovation paradigm speak primarily to innovation for India's domestic market, and not for global markets. By the same token, global companies like GE have research and development centres in India which produce intellectual property that is used globally. Despite successes by export-dependent industries in India, world perception clearly tilts toward that frugal innovation paradigm for India. While practical innovation or 'jugaad' in India may be lauded, and may even be termed as important for domestic markets, India's competitiveness as a global innovator lies in generating export-competitive innovation. India's best chances to make its mark on innovation may be in cleantech and other disruptive technologies that can improve the quality of life for the world's poor while enriching their inventors and investors. One such invention along that vein, a low-cost, durable, prosthesis known as the Jaipur foot, has restored function to amputees the world over and is probably the best-known Indian innovation to have found a global market. A paper on the Indian perspective on Innovation and Invention is placed at Annexure 8.

The Food Revolution

India has come a long way since independence when it was a low-income food-deficient country. Today the country is not only self-sufficient in rice and wheat, it also exports a range of food products and at any given time has up to 60 million tonnes of food grain buffer stocks. In a country as large as India it required visionaries like Mr MS Swaminathan, father of India's green revolution, and Mr BG Kurien, the father of India's white revolution to play a catalytic role in India's progress in the areas of crop and animal production and food security. These two revolutionary ideas of India have contributed greatly to the Indian success story. From 130 million tonnes in 1980, India's food grain production has risen to over 245 million tonnes in 2012. With Operation Flood, milk production rose to 113 million tonnes from about 35 million tonnes in 1980, also making it one of the largest employers of rural people, especially women. Fish production has also grown substantially. Employing over 15 million people, India is now a major fish exporter. Development of water resources for irrigation has underpinned crop production. However, water scarcity and falling water tables have been a key concern in recent years. On the positive side, this has led to awareness that water is an exhaustible resource. As a result, the importance of judicious use of water is being increasingly recognised. India has gone well beyond the realm of food production, covering issues like access to food and nutrition, livelihood, rural development and sustainable agriculture. With the looming impact of climate change and outbreaks of new strains of pests the requirements have become even more complex. A paper on the India's Food Revolution is placed at Annexure 9.

Panchayati Raj

Independence made India free. Democracy made Indian people

free. A free people are a people who are governed by their will and ruled with their consent. A free people are a people who participate in decisions affecting their lives and their destinies. The single greatest event in the evolution of democracy in India was the enactment of the Constitution which established democracy in Parliament and in the state Legislature. The historic, revolutionary Panchayati Raj Bill takes the place alongside that great event as the enshrinement in the constitution of democracy at the grassroots. The Panchayats have the same sanctity as is enjoyed by parliament and the state Legislature and the doors are opened for the participation in democratic institution. The Ministry of Panchayati Raj is the nodal body governing the Gram Panchayat system. The ministry has oversight of all state Panchayat bodies. The Panchayat, according to the Indian administrative code, is a form of government where a rural administrative entity is responsible for its own affairs. The evolution of Panchayati Raj in India is of immense interest to the developing as well as the developed countries across the world. The large size and immense canvass, the scope of activities, the large participation of women in local self-government are matters of their interest. Ministry of Panchayati Raj has taken several initiatives interacting with other similar bodies and Governments internationally, both to learn from their experience and contribute to the increasing body of common knowledge of various facets of devolution. The Ministry has signed memorandums of understanding with Switzerland, Indonesia and Norway. Details of Panchayati Raj are placed at Annexure 10.

Micro Small and Medium Enterprises

The Micro, Small and Medium Enterprises (MSMEs) sector contributes significantly to manufacturing, output, employment and exports of India. It is estimated that in terms of value, the sector accounts for about 45 per cent of the manufacturing output and 40 per cent of the total exports of the country. The sector is estimated to employ about 69 million persons in over 26 million units throughout the country. There are about 6,000 products ranging from traditional to high-tech items which are being manufactured by

MSMEs in the country. The sector provides maximum opportunities for both self-employment and jobs outside agricultural sectors. India has signed Memorandum of Understanding with a number of friendly foreign countries. Details of Micro Small and Medium Enterprises are placed at Annexure11.

Non Governmental Organisations

NGOs in India are working in various fields. Three Indian NGOs received the Red Ribbon Awards for outstanding community leadership and action in the fight against HIV/AID. These NGOs are People Like Us, Sangh Mitra and Sankalp Rehabilitation Trust. The UN has awarded General Consultative Status to Sulabh International for their pioneering work in developing environment friendly public toilet system. The General Consultative Status is the highest status given to an NGO within the UN System. A prominent Indian NGO, Chintan, was presented the US first Innovation Award for the empowerment women and girls. The award was given for its effort in training and organizing waste pickers and eliminating child labour. Some other internationally famous NGOs are SOS Children's Village, Help Age India, Sargam Sanstha, Smile Foundation, Give India, Lepra Society, Udaan, Deepalaya, Uday Foundation, Karm Yog and Pratham.

It is estimated that about 25,000 to 30,000 NGOs are active in India. One problem with NGOs in India, as with NGOs anywhere else in the world, has been the increasing dependency on governmental funds or donations from external (foreign) donors like the World Bank. This dependent relationship has resulted in a lack of voluntary initiative. Only a few NGOs may volunteer to operate a roster without government support.

Monitoring of Non-Government Organisations. The NGOs, which are registered under the Society's registration act, are required to submit an Annual Report, Audited Accounts and nominal role of their management committee. A public trust submits annual audited accounts and balance sheet to their registering authority. NGOs registered as non-profit making companies, are monitored as procedures laid down in the Company Law. The NGOs receiving Government aid or grant are subject to regular monitoring by the concerned ministry/department. It is mandatory for NGOs to file their income tax returns and follow the norms of financial propriety. The NGOs receiving foreign aid are required to register under Foreign Contribution Regulation Act.

Spiritual Aspect of CIVCAP

We customarily measure the cost of any conflict/violence or disaster, natural or otherwise, in terms of money, lost production and number of civilians, soldiers and/or militants killed. But the most painful and costly legacy of conflict of any kind is the individual human suffering – the emotional/spiritual breakdown! Do we realize that the psychological wounds are worse than physical ones? We read about combatants returning from war zone being traumatized but what about the trauma and the psychological stress faced by the civilians who continue to live in the war ravaged zones? Psychological support has to be given to people to rehabilitate them in the true sense. Just as Phoenix rises from its own ashes, they have to rise to fresh challenges of life again from the depth of hopelessness created by the trauma of violence / conflict / disaster. A simple and practical program is needed, besides other aids, to assist people to get back their self-esteem, dignity and faith in themselves. Yes, we need to factor in the spiritual dimension to the civilian capacity building that we talk of. Spirituality is the intangible dimension of peace building. A paper on the Spiritual Dimension of Civilian Capacity Building is placed at Annexure 12.

CHAPTER 5

CONCLUSION

India's unique combination of being the largest democracy in the world with a strong tradition of respect for rule of law and the successful experience in nation building makes it particularly relevant in the context of twenty-first century peace building. The post conflict situations and, indeed, those of prolonged conflict demand that serious attention is paid to building basic government structures and providing basic services, without which the chances of lapsing into conflict multiply manifold. India's experience in transforming a colonial legacy into a modern, dynamic nation that is both a democracy and a rapidly growing economy made Indian peacekeepers instinctively understand that no peace can be effective unless it is accompanied by growth of local institutions.

The Government of India's ITEC Programme and its corollary SCAAP provide 158 countries in Asia, East Europe, Central Asia, Africa, Latin America, the Caribbean as well as Pacific and Small Island countries an opportunity to share in the Indian developmental experience in various fields. Consequent to the wide variety of activities under the ITEC programme, there is now a visible and growing awareness among other countries about the competence of India as a provider of technical know-how and expertise as well as training opportunities, consultancy services and feasibility studies. Over the years, this assistance programme has generated immense goodwill and substantive cooperation among the developing countries.

It is the flagship programme of the Indian Government's technical cooperation effort, not only because of its wide geographical coverage but also for innovative forms of technical cooperation. Being essentially bilateral in nature, ITEC is about cooperation and partnership for mutual benefit. It is demand-driven and response-oriented. With the plethora of skills covered under this programme, it is opined that the United Nations associate with this programme under a capacity providing MoU and address to identify candidates in specialised categories. This would help exploit a well working system of capacity provision while obviating the need to set up a new civilian capacity provider. While a majority of Indian technical assistance and capacity building programmes have been envisaged essentially as bilateral programmes, there have been instances when resources have been used for financing technical cooperation programmes conceived in regional and inter-regional context.

As we enter into 21st Century, there are many in India as also in the international arena, who perceive a more dynamic and significant role for India in the field of international relations, including the maintenance of international peace and security. This obviously means greater role in various organs of the United Nations. If India is to fulfil such a role with any degree of credibility, it is inevitable that it accepts the responsibilities that go with such an enhanced, high profile role. India can do this by offering our acknowledged expertise in various areas of United Nations activities and most importantly in peacekeeping. India must make most of its proven experience and professionalism in this field and put it to good use for maintenance of international peace and security and help the conflict affected countries in their peace building, state building and nation building efforts.[14]

---

14   For the Honour of India, ibid.

CHAPTER 6

RECOMMENDATIONS FOR INDIAN CIVILIAN CAPACITY PROVISION

The study referred to a number of reports on various aspects of the Civilian Capacity, consulted a variety of experts, and interacted with various Ministries, Institutions, and Departments of the Government of India. The recommendations for Indian Civilian Capacity Provision are enumerated in the succeeding paragraphs.

1.   India should continue to support nationally led plans for peace consolidation. National actors and institutions of the affected country should be the primary source of civilian capacity. International capacity should be used as the mechanism of last resort.

2.   The Peace Keeping Missions should involve themselves in building local capacity for provision of basic administration and essential services. Civilian capacities are critical in this endeavor and their presence in the Peace Keeping Missions should be ensured. Peacekeepers should provide hub center for all peace building process and activities.

3.   Force generation model of DPKO should be used to generate civilian capacity for peace building. The United Nations should strengthen its outreach to India building on the successful Peacek Keeping Model. All requirements of peace building must be routed through the Ministry of External Affairs.

4.   The United Nations and the member countries should make greater use of existing mechanisms and use them for deploying needed civilian capacity for Peace Building.

5.   India should continue to engage itself proactively and in

constructive manner to help realize goals of enhancing civilian capacity in the post conflict situations under United Nations as well as on bilateral basis.

6.   There is an international shift in many fields towards sourcing capabilities from global South. This shift has been driven by sound economic and functional consideration. United Nations should source the needed Civilian Capacity from the developing countries like India which has a vast reservoir of Civilian Capacity in almost all fields.

7.   The recruitment model should give primacy to a partnership with the Government of Member States. The needed Civilian Capacity should be found primarily out of Government officials on secondment basis. The short falls in the needed capacity should be obtained from non-governmental sectors.

8.   The Government of India should develop a mechanism to ensure that the conflict affected countries get the civilian support, what they need and when they need. The demands should be need driven.

9.   Following a specific request for support, member states provide military or police personnel to the United Nations and are reimbursed at a standard rate, agreed in letter of assist. This mechanism should be extended to provide teams of civilians from member states.

10.   The Government of India should establish a legal and administrative mechanism to enable deployment of needed civilian capacity from Government, semi-government and non-government sectors.

11.   The administrative mechanism should ensure that personnel with needed expertise are allowed to maintain link and lien on their regular career while they provide their services to United Nations or to friendly countries on bilateral basis.

12.   The Ministry of External Affairs (MEA) should proactively

publicise and offer Civilian Capacity to UN and needy countries without waiting for a request being made by them.

13.   The MEA should act as a single point contact for UN, Countries needing Civilian Capacity, UN Missions, various Agencies and Funds and non-governmental organizations operating in the conflict affected countries. The requirement for help and support should be received and considered by the MEA (DPA) for its desirability keeping in view factors like assessment of national interest in a given situation, adherence to the principles of peace building, bilateral relations, consent of all parties, regional equations, public perception in host countries, safety and security of personnel, desirability and viability of the mission.

14.   The request found desirable should be passed on to a Nodal Ministry for Civilian Capacity. The study group recommends that the MHA should be the Nodal Ministry for providing Civilian Capacity. The Ministry should have a Civilian Capacity Cell (C3). The cell should forward the requirement to the lead agency of the concerned cluster. For details of the proposed clusters and their lead agencies refer to Annexure 6.

15.   The lead agency should carry out a feasibility and availability analysis of the needed civilian capacity in the Government departments, semi-government sector and autonomous bodies. Details of the volunteer civilian experts who could be made available for deployment should be forwarded to the MEA where necessary political clearance is given and other administrative and legal procedures for deployment should be completed.

16.   In case the lead agency does not find suitable volunteers in the Government / semi-government sector, it should outsource the requirement to non- governmental organizations/corporate sectors.

17.   The lead agencies should maintain a roster of civilian experts available for deployment in the UN Missions abroad.

18.   The lead agencies should also outsource the responsibility

of maintaining roster of civilian experts to suitable Government Departments, Autonomous Bodies and voluntary non-governmental organisations.

19.   Under the ITEC programme, Indian experts are deputed to friendly countries. ITEC should also deploy experts on the UN Peace Building Missions.

20.   EC should provide expertise in areas or electoral management, administration, electoral reforms and electoral laws. The EC has already signed MOUs with a number of countries and the UN. Similar MOUs should be signed for deployment of exerts in the conflict affected countries.

21.   India is the only country which has a dedicated force standby for disaster relief. This force should be made available on voluntary basis to the countries in distress for providing relief and rehabilitation.

22.   NIDM should help in building capacities of the conflict affected countries.

23.   The CDC exports capabilities of consultants in various fields and maintains a database of the consultants in India. The Centre should in identifying consultants and experts available for deployment in UN Peace Building Missions.

24.   India has a vigorous NGO sector. This resource should be harnessed for identifying volunteers and maintaining rosters.

25.   **Civilian Capacity Clusters and Lead Agencies**. A compilation of civilian capacity clusters and lead agencies as applicable in India is placed at Annexure 13.

PEACEKEEPERS AS PEACE BUILDERS

Over the years some important Qualitative changes have taken place in peacekeeping operations. Most of the recent conflicts have taken place, or are taking place, within states. The combatants in such conflicts are not national armies, but para-military forces, militias, and irregulars. The larger tragedies in these conflicts are that civilians are main victims (90% now as against 10% earlier). In many cases, states institutions have collapsed. In a few cases there are no governments. As a result humanitarian emergencies have forced the international community to intervene. This is why demands on UN peacekeeping have gone well beyond traditional peace keeping. They now encompass activities like disarming and demobilization of troops and armed para-militaries or irregulars, promotion of national reconciliation, restoration of effective government and rule of law mechanisms, the organization and monitoring of elections, provision of broader support to humanitarian aid missions, including escort of relief convoys, and protection of the safe areas. Over the years, the UN peacekeeping missions have become more expensive, more complex and more dangerous. The peacekeepers have performed with distinction under the changed circumstances. They have undertaken the following peace building activities in various missions.

Cambodia: UN Transitional Authority, UNTAC 1992-93

In January 1990, the UN Security Council started a series of high level meetings on Cambodia. These consultations called for major UN role in bringing peace to the country, which included the deployment of UN peacekeeping forces, the supervision of free elections and erection of an administrative infrastructure. UN Advance Mission in Cambodia (UNAMIC) was deployed. It was to prepare ground for deployment of peacekeeping mission called the

UN Transitional Authority in Cambodia (UNTAC). This peacekeeping mission included 3500 police personnel. There was a provision for up to 1,149 international civilian staff, 456 UNVs and 4830 local staff. The UNTAC mandate included the rehabilitation and reconstruction of the country.

The military component was required to maintain a secure environment for the registration of voters and actual conduct of election. The UNTAC was empowered to govern Cambodia during transitional period, overseeing its foreign affairs, national defence, finance, public security and information ministries.

Gaza: UN Emergency Force (UNEF) 1 (1956-57)

In the Gaza Strip the peacekeepers comprising of the Indian contingent had the most challenging responsibilities, which it shouldered with professionalism and efficiency. After the withdrawal of Israeli troops, the area did not any responsible local administration. Detachments of the Indian contingent took up positions in various population centres and involved themselves in assisting the local administration and providing sustenance to the local populace.

Lebanon: United Nations Interim Force, UNIFIL

The mission mandate for UNIFIL, inter alia, included "extend its assistance to help ensure humanitarian access to civilian populations and the voluntary and safe return of the displaced persons". The concept of operation envisaged:-

(a) Providing humanitarian assistance to the local population.

(b) Winning the hearts and minds of the local population.

(c) Working with the Lebanese Government to help them establish their authority and control in the area.

The Indian contingents in Lebanon were involved in humanitarian activities and the creation of local infrastructure through Quick Impact Projects. Most of these civilian activities were carried out in addition to the military task and were beyond the peacekeepers call of duty. The contingent worked hard to relieve the suffering of local population and worked within the mandate which stipulated that UNIFIL 'carry out, with the consent of Government of Lebanon, tasks in the humanitarian and administrative fields, to restore normal social and economic life in the area of operations and assist in ensuring the security of all inhabitants in the area without discrimination.

Medical care was given to poor and needy civilians. Indian medical contingent maintained the UNIFIL hospitals. They were extensively involved in immunization campaign. Many quick impact projects (QIPs) like vocational training to the youth and encouraging educational and sports activities were organized.

Congo: The Second UN Mission, MONUC

The eagerly awaited elections in Democratic Republic of Congo were held in two stages in July and October2006. To ensure that the election process was carried out peacefully, extensive contingency planning took place. Operation Rising Sun was undertaken by the peacekeepers to support the electoral process in the province.

Ever since its deployment in North Kivu province, 301 Brigade Group of India was actively involved in 'Winning Hearts and Minds' (WHAM) Campaign. This was primarily because it was the first UN force to be deployed in this sensitive reason. Because of the Indian peacekeepers deployment, a large number of refugees who had fled the violence and instability in North Kivu now began to return to their homes. Sustained interaction with local populace enabled Indian soldiers to identify and try to ameliorate the problems they faced. In this area, the troops were in place well before any of the aid agencies or NGOs arrived, and so had better sense of conditions on the ground. Indian troops had more advantage in that they were already familiar with WHAM strategies through earlier experience of counter insurgency operations in India itself. Units of the Indian contingent focused on the humanitarian aspects of the mission.

The peace keepers constructed a road to Kikingi village with active participation of 5,000 villagers. They helped in construction of a bridge and Hydel Power project. The peacekeepers centred on four key programmes: youth development, public awareness, public welfare, and quick impact projects.

Somalia: UN Operation UNOSOM II

On 3 March 1993 the UN Secretary General identified three main challenges for the UN peacekeepers in Somalia:-

(a) Facilitate voluntary return of 300,000 refugees and internally displaced persons.

(b) Help provide jobs and work for the many millions of unemployed Somalis including members of armed gangs, militias and various private armies.

(c) Assist in rebuilding of Somali society and rehabilitation of decayed infrastructure.

The mandate also included assisting in the rehabilitation of decayed infrastructure. The primary mission of the Indian contingent was to help create and maintain a stable environment in which political reconciliation and delivery of humanitarian aid could be safely undertaken. The contingent was also required to assist in economic development and humanitarian relief operations, and assist in restoration of judiciary.

The Indian Brigade group perceived humanitarian actions as one of the most important components of its operational activity. Conceptually, the humanitarian operations were directed towards winning the hearts and minds of local people, generating pride in all Somalis in their own country and sustainable assistance carried out by locals themselves. Although a number of NGOs were working in Somalia, large area of the country remained inaccessible to them. Indian peacekeepers were generally warmly greeted by locals Somalis villagers and town folks as coming from the land of 'MOAMMED GANDHI'.

A vital task Indian contingent addressed was to assist the Somalis in restoring 'national structures' that had completely collapsed during the civil war. To facilitate cooperation and harmony between various elements of civil society, including police judiciary, youth and clan chiefs, the peacekeepers engaged locals in mediation and conflict resolution. The Indian contingent assisted in restoring administrative machinery in most of the districts and regions. This included resuscitating administrative processes, retraining of police force and activating judicial systems at district and regional levels.

Rawanda : UN Assistance Mission, UNMIR

In August 1993, a UN reconnaissance mission visited Rwanda. On the basis of the mission's findings-that the Arusha Peace Agreement did not settle the violent conflict between the Government and the rebels who had ravaged the country since independence- the Secretary General submitted a report to the Security Council on 24 September 1993, calling for the creation of a UN Assistance Mission for Rwanda (UNAMIR). The proposed functions of UNAMIR, inter alia, included providing security for the repatriation pf Rwandese refugees and displaced persons and coordinating humanitarian assistance activities in conjunction with the relief operations.

A major humanitarian crisis developed after bloodbath in Rwanda, wherein nearly 2 million people were displaced and moved to hillside camps on Congolese-Rwandan border. UNMAR's mandate was expanded to ensure protection of refugees and civilians at risk, through the establishment and maintenance of safe heavens, and provision of security for relief operation to the extent possible.

Within the limited resources Indian peacekeepers carried out well coordinated humanitarian aid programmes. This included medical aid to the locals, help in conducting school examinations and help to a number of NGOs. They helped in rehabilitation of orphans by providing help to orphanages.

Ethiopia and Eritrea: UN Mission, UNMEE 2000

As of March 2000, it was estimated that over 370,000 Eritreans and approximately 350,000 Ethiopians had been affected by the war. The humanitarian crisis in parts of Ethiopia was exacerbated by the severe draught. The Secretary General's special envoy Ms Bertini, after her survey of the area and discussions with the Government officials, believed that famine in the Horn of Africa could be averted with swift international response. She noted five priority areas: water, basic medicine, food aid, security and technical support in transport and infrastructure to ensure distribution of aid. According to MS Bertini, 'the international community has a rare opportunity of prevention'. She add, however, that 'timings is absolutely critical' to prevent a disaster. A United Nations Task Force was established to deal with the emergency and long term food needs in the Horn of Africa.

The Indian peacekeepers also focused on humanitarian activities related to water management and medical treatment of both humans and cattle. Thousand of youths were trained in subjects ranging from computer to automobile and machinery repairs, carpentry and basic medical and dental treatment. The Engineer component carried out multifarious tasks in the mission. These included construction roads and tracks, water management in draught prone areas, digging shallow and deep wells and rain water harvesting. Making play grounds, feeding in schools, and tree plantation were extremely popular projects.

Winning over hearts and minds of the local civilian population through humanitarian aid has been one of the most important elements of Indian peacekeeping operations, and UNMEE was no exception.

Sudan: UN Mission, UNMIS

UNMIS was established as a special political mission to assist the peace efforts. The mission mandate included the following:-

(a) Promote inclusiveness of peace.

(b) Reorganise the police forces and promote the rule of law.

(c) Promote election awareness among the local population.

(d) Facilitate and coordinate voluntary return of refugees and internally displaced persons to their homes

(e) Establish a safe and secure environment, in which humanitarian assistance, can take place.

(f) Assist the parties in de-mining.

Apart from performing their assigned tasks listed above, the peacekeepers provided much needed humanitarian aid to local population. They helped the victims of jaundice, cholera and Hepatitis-E. Normal activities for winning over the hearts and mind of the people continued. The Indian contingent played role of true ambassadors of their country going to the rescue of local inhabitants in their hour of crisis and provided much needed relief to them.

Angola: UN Verification and Observers Missions, UNAVEM I-III

UNAVEM was primarily an Observer Group. For UNAVEM II the mandate was enlarged to include:-

(a) Monitor neutrality of the police.

(b) Provide technical advice o0n electoral matters and supervision of elections.

The mandate of UNAVEN III was further expanded and it, inter alia, included the following tasks:-

(a) The verification and monitoring of the neutrality of the Angolan police force.

(b) Disarming of civilians.

(c) Quartering of the Government rapid reaction police.

(d) Making security arrangements for UNITA leaders.

(e) Coordinating, facilitating and supporting humanitarian work directly linked to the peace process particularly those relating to quartering and demoblisation of troops and their reintegration in civil life.

(f) Participating in mine clearing activities.

UNAVEM III was to inspect arrangements for the second round of the presidential election, and to formally declare that these were correct, complete and proper. The UN mission was to closely monitor and validate the electoral process.

The Indian peacekeepers adopted very human approach towards local civilians. They gave vocational training to the demoblised soldiers, made market places, and organized sports meets. The veterinary teams treated nearly 50,000 livestock. The Engineer component restored essential infrastructure which was destroyed during long years of war. They repaired and reopened major roads.

Mozambique: UN Operation, ONUMOZ

ONUMOZ mandate included providing technical assistance and facilitating humanitarian assistance operations, in particular those relating to refugees, internally displaced persons, demoblised military personnel and affected local civil population.

The Indian peacekeeper constructed tracks and training centers. They made assembly areas for demobilised soldiers. The peacekeepers launched a humanitarian assistance programme to help 3.7 million people displaced by the bitter war to resettle in their communities. The Indian engineers and military observers contributed significantly to these vital nation building activities.

Sierra Leone: UN Mission, UNAMSIL

UNAMSIL mandate included:-

(a) Facilitate delivery of humanitarian assistance and support the operation of the UN civilian official.

(b) Provide support, as requested, to the elections.

Apart from their operational role the Indian peacekeepers took an active part in humanitarian activities. They maintained roads, provided safe drinking water, provided medical assistance and distributed food. They organized 'Kick Polio out of Sierra Leone'. The medical team faced new challenges due to some tropical diseases like Lassa fever and Tombo Fly Disease. Lassa fever had a mortality rate of 90%. Besides these activities, normal civic action programmes continued.

Afghanistan

India has no military presence in Afghanistan. An estimated 3,000 Indian nationals in Afghanistan work for reconstruction companies, international aid agencies or are Indian government employees working at the consulates and embassies. As part of its humanitarian mission, India established field clinics and a children's hospital. It also runs a program providing midday-meals to about 2 million Afghan schoolchildren.

In the construction sector, an important work constructed by Indians is the 217 kilometre Delaram–Zaranj Highway, or Route 606 by Indian construction agencies in Southern Afghanistan, the completion of which in August 2009 has given a viable alternative route for duty free movement of goods through the Chahabar port in Iran to Afghanistan. Road building has been a prominent component of India reconstruction aid – over 700 kilometers of roads have been built in the preceding eight years. The hallmark project of the Indian aid effort is a majestic domed edifice costing $125 million for the Afghan Parliament. The Government of India has also provided assistance in strengthening institutions and human resource development. Scholarships were provided in 2009 for 700 Afghan citizens while Afghan public servants were granted access to government training institutions in India for periods ranging from days to six months. The Indian government furthermore provides scholarships to more than 1,000 Afghan students per year.

The widespread support in the Pashtun heartland for an even greater Indian role in rebuilding the Afghan economy and society is "striking". In 2011 India and Afghanistan signed the Strategic Partnership Agreement which would allow India to train and equip Afghan security forces.

India is one of the largest donors to Afghanistan, investing in the economy, humanitarian aid, education, development, construction and electrical projects. It has committed a $ 2.3 billion aid programme.

It is evident from the above details that peacekeepers are the first peace builders. In the current missions also the Indian peacekeepers continue to undertake Civic Action Programme to 'WIN OVER THE HEART AND MIND OF THE PEOPLE. They should be provided with adequate resources to undertake meaningful peace building activities.

(This annexure is based on the data and details given in 'For the Honour of India, A History of Indian Peacekeeping' by Lieutenant General Satish Nambiar, PVSM, AVSM, VrC (retd), published by Centre for Armed Forces Historical Research, United Service Institute of India.)

Annexure 2

CIVILIAN CAPACITY/ ASSISTANCE PROVIDED BY INDIA TO VARIOUS COUNTRIES BETWEEN 2007-2012

Countries	Trade /trade assistance	Training	Projects	Deputation of Indian Experts	Gift & Dona-tions	Capacity Building
Afghanistan	$2 billion, trade assistance	675 trainees trained under Indian Technical and Educational Co-operation (ITEC), training scholarships for Afghan public servants .	Infrastructure humanitarian development projects along with education and capacity development.	20 Indian Civil Servants served as coaches and mentors under Capacity for Afghan Public Administration programmes	675 long-term university scholarships	
Algeria	Trade of $ 3.4 billion	150 officials are trained	Projects under Power, Oil, Construction and Pharma	2500 Indians working in different fields	1 million as humanitarian assistance	

Countries	Trade /trade assistance	Training	Projects	Deputation of Indian Experts	Gift & Donations	Capacity Building
Angola	Credit of US$ 40 million.		Three credit lines of US$ 5, 10 and 13.8 million for agricultural equipment and Indian tractors	The State Bank of India which opened its Representative Office in Luanda	Rehabilitation of CFM	Setting up an Industrial park and US$15 million for setting up a cotton ginning and spinning plant and construction of a cement plant in Sumbe
Armenia	Grant of US$ 5 million	35 Slots under ITEC, National Statistical Service underwent a training programme in India	A project to create/upgrade computer labs in 72 schools in Tavush Province is currently under process		US$ 2.2 million cash and US$ 1.1 million relief supplies were donated by India.	US $ 215,000/- for the restoration of a dilapidated school building in a relatively remote rural area.
Barbados	Trade of US$ 5.63Millions	11 Scholarships under ITEC to Barbados	Projects in information technology, cotton cultivation and textile industry			Larsen and Toubro has built a $ 30-million stadium in Barbados.

Countries	Trade /trade assistance	Training	Projects	Deputation of Indian Experts	Gift & Donations	Capacity Building
Benin	$ 15 million LOC	20 Seats under ITEC	Projects under industry,	3 Member team from Central Institute of Agriculture Engineering, Bhopal visited Benin	Donated 100 tractors and half a million dollars in cash for flood relief	An IT Centre of Excellence and a Centre of Demonstration of Technology were to be set up with Indian grants
Bolivia	Cash contribution of US $ 200,000	5 Slots annually for civilian training	JSPL investing about US $ 2.1 billion over a period of 8 years		India gave a cash contribution of US $ 200,000 to Bolivia as a relief measure in the wake of floods, donated medicines worth US$ 200,000	
Bosnia & Herzegovina	Trade of US$ 50 million	Two slots under ITEC	Projects under the Ispat Group of India			Establish an IT training centre, sends its diplomats to attend the PCFD courses

Countries	Trade /trade assistance	Training	Projects	Deputation of Indian Experts	Gift & Donations	Capacity Building
Burkina Faso	LOC of US$ 30.97 million	Two professionals were trained under the IAFS	Farmers Project has been approved for setting up a Tomato Processing Factory	Expert farmers to demonstrate technology of rice growing,	Consignment of medicines and US$ 213,356 was donated to Burkina Faso as India's contribution towards flood relief assistance	Construction/ equipping of National Post Office, rural electrification, set up two projects viz., Vocational Training Centre / Incubation Centre (VTC/IC) and Vocational Training Centre of Barefoot College
Burundi	Line of Credit of US$ 80 million	30 Slots under ITEC	An African e-Network Project and establishment of cluster bio-mass gasifier system	Team of experts from the implementing agency to undertake feasibility studies for bio-mass gasifier system	Consignments of medicines for distribution in refugee camps	20MW Kabu hydroelectric project also offered to set-up an Information Technology Centre in Burundi.

Countries	Trade /trade assistance	Training	Projects	Deputation of Indian Experts	Gift & Donations	Capacity Building
Cambodia	LOC of $ 1.7 million for Asian Traditional Textiles Museum	943 civilian training slots and 98 defence training slots.	Electric transmission lines, irrigation and installation of water pumps projects	1500 Indian nationals in different sectors		Entrepreneurship Development Centre ,Centre for English Language Training
Cameroon	$ 37.65 million Line of Credit	Cameroonian diplomat attended a one-month PCFD course.31 slots under ITEC	Indian investments in oil and mining, telecom, fertilizers, oil & gas, agriculture & food processing, forestry, IT and railways		Gifted 60 tractors and agricultural tools	Contract for exploration of bauxite in Adamawa region, Cameroon signed the Pan-African e-Network Project with TCIL
Cape Verde	Line of Credit of US$ 5 million	20 Slots under ITEC	Project documentation for the desalination plant		Assistance of US$ 50,000 to fight dengue fever	Refurbishment of a healthcare centre in Cape Verde ,setting up of a Technology Park

Countries	Trade /trade assistance	Training	Projects	Deputation of Indian Experts	Gift & Donations	Capacity Building
Central African Republic	$ 29.5 million credit	English Language Training Institute	Cement plant project and US $ 5.5 million for supply of 100 buses,	50 trading and construction activities.		Two learning stations, Tele-education, Telemedicine and Farm Science Centre to be developed.
Chad	LOC of $ 40.32 million & another of US$ 50 million	20 Slots under ITEC	Projects under infrastructure, transport, energy, mining, ICT, health and agriculture.		Donated 5,000 metric tonnes of rice to Chad	A mini-cement plant is under consideration, Bicycle manufacturing plant, plant for manufacturing and assembly of agricultural tractors, power tillers, trailers and implements, steel billet plant and rolling mill, cotton yarn plant and a fruit juice plant.

Countries	Trade /trade assistance	Training	Projects	Deputation of Indian Experts	Gift & Donations	Capacity Building
Commonwealth of Dominica	Trade of US$ 1.57 million	Ten slots have been annually earmarked for CD.	Dominica has sought Indian expertise in the field of solar and geo-thermal energy	Scientist (Horticulture) from National Research Centre for Banana, visited Dominica		Going o set-up an IT Centre of Excellence
Democratic Republic of Congo	US$ 33.5 million in2006, US$ 25 million in 2008 US$ 168 million in 2011	60 DRC officials were selected for short and medium term training courses in India	US$ 33.5 million for cement plant and acquisition of buses for transport sector, US$ 25 million for Rural Water Supply Project and Kakobola Hydro-Electric Project		60 "Sonalika" tractors with accessories & spares worth US$ 0.66 million, US$ 1 million for supply of medicines, IT Centre of Excellence in Kinshasa and 3 learning stations under the Hole-in-Wall Computer Education project	Congolese women were trained in solar electrification and water courses, setting up of Human Settlement Centres. Vocational Training Centre (VTC) in DRC, Soil, Water and Tissue Testing Laboratory under AIFS-II.

Countries	Trade /trade assistance	Training	Projects	Deputation of Indian Experts	Gift & Donations	Capacity Building
Democratic Republic of Congo	$ 33.5 million for cement, $ 25 million for Rural Water Supply Project	60 DRC officials for training courses and 10 scholarships were given.	Mining of copper, cobalt and diamond Projects in DRC	7,000 Indians or PIOs in service sector and trading-	Donated 60 "Sonalika" tractor and $ 1 million for supply of medicines;	9 DRC officials under IAFS
Djibouti	Trade of US$ 371.04Million		Pan-African e-Network Agreement signed between TCIL and Djibouti		Humanitarian assistance worth US$ 1 million in the form of wheat, rice and medicine	600 TPD cement plant at Ali Sabieh, Indian Naval Ships call at Djibouti port regularly
Dominican Republic	Trade of US $ 100 million.	30 Slots under ITEC	IT, Pharmaceuticals, and infrastructure projects.			NIIT signed a MoU with Cyber Park of Santo Domingo to establish IT training centre.

Countries	Trade /trade assistance	Training	Projects	Deputation of Indian Experts	Gift & Donations	Capacity Building
Egypt	Trade of US$ 3090.86 million	101 trainee were trained under ITEC programme, 21 under IAFS, Capacity building and AARDO programmes.	Cooperation in the field of agricultural research and production of PVC and caustic soda			India launched a Pan African e-Network Project, Centre for Indian Culture in Cairo ,50 Indian companies operating in Egypt
El Salvador	Line of Credit of US$ 15 million	30 ITEC slots	Projects under pharmaceuticals, fabrics, organic chemicals,	Deputation of 2-3 experts under ITEC to El Salvador in field of coconut farming, Tropical Fruits & Microfinance are under advanced stage of finalisation.	Donated medicines worth Rs 5 lakhs, 18 Bajaj three wheelers and cash donation of US$ 250,000 as humanitarian aid	IT Training Centre has been set up.

Countries	Trade /trade assistance	Training	Projects	Deputation of Indian Experts	Gift & Donations	Capacity Building
Eritrea	Trade of US $1.28 billion	Scholarships through the Indian Technical and Economic Cooperation program (ITEC)	Projects under inland fisheries and aquaculture.	100 Indian agricultural experts were deputed to Eritrea to help increase agricultural productivity and production		India offered assistance in its legislative drafting process, capacity building assistance in agriculture, medicine and education.
Ethiopia	$ 4.78 billion investment	135 training slots	Projects under commercial agriculture, electrification and sugar industry.	Consultancy to the Ethiopian Revenue and Customs Authority, experts in protocol and diplomatic training, experts in soil testing and computerization of land records.		Developing Tele Education Centre, Tele-Medicine Centre, Central Leather Research Institute.

Countries	Trade /trade assistance	Training	Projects	Deputation of Indian Experts	Gift & Dona-tions	Capacity Building
Fiji	US$ 50.4 million Line of Credit	25 Slots under the ITEC and 10 slots under the TCS	Project for up gradation of sugar industry in Fiji		Assistance of US$100,000 and contributed US$ 100,000 to the Prime Minister's National Disaster, Relief and Rehabilitation fund	Funds given for purchase of 5 Toyota Cars for Fiji Police, 200 sewing Machines, supply of 5 Ambulances for hospitals and supply of 134 Water Tanks
Gabon	Credit of US$ 14.45 million	15 ITEC slots have been earmarked	Implemented the Pan African e-network project. Tele-education, Tele-medicine and VVIP connectivity has been set up under this.			A Vocational Training Centre would be set up in Gabon and also an Entrepreneurship Development Institute (EDI)

Countries	Trade /trade assistance	Training	Projects	Deputation of Indian Experts	Gift & Donations	Capacity Building
Gambia	Credit of US$ 6.7 million and another of US $ 10 million	40 Slots under SCAAP and has 8 slots under ICCR's General Cultural Scholarship Scheme (GCSS).	The Pan-African E-Network Project, implemented by Telecommunications Consultants India Limited (TCIL)		A grant of US $ five hundred thousand to the Republic of The Gambia for providing equipment in the health and education sectors	A tractor assembly plant, the construction of National Assembly Building complex, A Solar Electrification Project in two villages and a Vocational Training Centre is planned

Countries	Trade /trade assistance	Training	Projects	Deputation of Indian Experts	Gift & Donations	Capacity Building
Ghana	Rs 38.53 million	125 slots under Indian Technical and Economic Cooperation (ITEC).	Projects dealing with fisheries, waste management, railway equipment, agro-processing, fire-tenders	Consultancy in construction, manufacturing, trading, services and tourism and in areas such as steel cement, plastics, pharmaceuticals, ICT, agro-processing and agricultural machinery, electrical equipment, chemicals,		Centre of Excellence for Training in Information Technology
Guatemala	India has provided assistance of US$250,000	The number of ITEC slots for Guatemala is 10.	Projects under hydro-electric field and alternative fuels		An Indian donation of US$50,000 worth of medicines was given and India donated 36 Bajaj three-wheelers	Has set up an IT Training Centre in San Carlos University

Countries	Trade /trade assistance	Training	Projects	Deputation of Indian Experts	Gift & Dona-tions	Capacity Building
Guinea	LOC of US$ 8.51 mn	25 Slots under ITEC			Donated fifty electric trans-formers	Implementation of PAN African e-Net-work project
Guinea Bissau	LOC of US$ 25 million for Guinea Bissau	3C Slots for train-ing ITEC		An expert in the area of rice cultivation visited Guinea Bissau		Assist in a Solar Power project.
Guyana	A Line of Credit of US$ 25.5 million and an additional US$ 50 million was offered	50 Slots annually under ITEC		A team of experts conducted a fea-sibility study for a deep water port in Guyana.		Scholarships are also offered under Cultural and Commonwealth schemes
Haiti	A relief of US $ 500,000 annually for three years till 2011	12 Slots under ITEC programme and Haitian diplo-mats have been attending PCFD course			Aid of Rs Ten Million and donated medi-cines worth US $ 50000 as humanitarian assistance	The new President has requested that dwelling units 500-1000 may be devel-oped by India

Countries	Trade /trade assistance	Training	Projects	Deputation of Indian Experts	Gift & Donations	Capacity Building
Indonesia	Bilateral trade of US $ 16.16 billion	75 Slots under ITEC AND 1300 Indonesian officials have attended training programmes i	Companies have substantial investments in the textiles, steel, automotive, banking and resources sectors		Donated US$ 2 million in relief assistance, Indian assistance of $ 100,000 for those affected by Mt Merapi eruptions	Aditya Birla group has a viscose fibre plant and downstream units, Essar has a cold-rolled steel mill near Jakarta and Jindal Stainless Steel has a factory in Surabaya.
Jamaica	LOC of US$ 7.5 million	15 slots annually to Jamaica under the ITEC programme		Deputed a faculty of 3 computer experts	An assistance of US$ 200,000 in medicines and medical supplies and donated US$ 300,000 as humanitarian assistance	Set up an IT Centre and also provided the entire hardware, software and training modules

Countries	Trade /trade assistance	Training	Projects	Deputation of Indian Experts	Gift & Donations	Capacity Building
Jordan	Bilateral trade of US$ 1.16 billion	20 Slots under ITEC	An MoU on cooperation in Science and Technology was signed			500 Jordanian students pursuing studies in different universities in India.
Kenya	Trade of US$ 61.6 million	100 Scholarships for professional training in the Indian Technical & Economic sector,12 in IAFS training programmes	Projects under pharmaceuticals, steel products, machinery, yarn, vehicles and power transmission equipment.	Consultancy in petroleum refining, telecom, automobiles, IT, pharmaceuticals	Humanitarian assistance of US$ 8 million to the countries affected by famine and drought	

Countries	Trade /trade assistance	Training	Projects	Deputation of Indian Experts	Gift & Donations	Capacity Building
Laos	Trade of US $ 18 million.	210 Scholarships to Laos nationals under ITEC, 150 slots for Lao defence personnel in English, Computers and Basic Tactics.	Projects under agriculture machinery, irrigation pumps, garment raw-material, drugs and pharmaceuticals, machinery, paints and varnishes, textiles, sports and electrical goods			Developing 115 KV Paksong-Jiangxi-Bangyo transmission line project in Champassak province, development of irrigation schemes in Champassak province
Laos	LOC amounting to US$ 132.89	210 Scholarships through ITEC [150 slots] and the TCS Colombo Plan [40 slots],	Eucalyptus pulp and plantation project and an iron ore mine project, set up an IT centre in Vientiane			Constructed 115 KV Transmission Line from Ban-Na to Attapeu, The Nam Song 7.5 MW hydropower project, development of irrigation schemes in Champasak province

Countries	Trade /trade assistance	Training	Projects	Deputation of Indian Experts	Gift & Donations	Capacity Building
Lebanon	Trade of US$ 354 million	54 Candidates have been trained in cooperative banking, journalism, diplomacy, legislative drafting, computers, auditing etc.		Stationed Indian battalion has 863 Indian troops and 14 doctors serving in the UNIFIL.25 Indian armed forces personnel are deployed at the UNIFIL HQs at Naqoura	Medical advice and assistance, veterinary aid and technical support to schools. It has also provided the Jaipur Foot to mine victims in the villages in South Lebanon.	Assistance to the tune of US$ 600,000 for re-habilitation and reconstruction of the Nahr-al-Bared Palestinian refugee camp
Lesotho	One time grant of Rs 86.99 million	The Indian Army Training Team (IATT) stationed in Lesotho ,56 ITEC slots in civil training	Projects under small industries, Rural Development	4 Indian agricultural experts/ technicians, an Indian Expert to advise the Director of the Lesotho College of Agriculture	Donated US$ 50,000 worth of anti-retroviral HIV/AIDS medicine and 5000 tons each of wheat flour and rice and large number of books to the National Library Lesotho in 2004.	An advanced Centre for IT has been set up by India at Lerotholi Polytechnic.

Countries	Trade /trade assistance	Training	Projects	Deputation of Indian Experts	Gift & Donations	Capacity Building
Liberia	SDR 11.15 million and US$ 2 million aid	Twenty slots are provided under the ITEC programme, India Africa Forum Summit training 22 candidates	Projects under pharmaceuticals, transportation equipment, steel and plastic products and iron ore mine.	150 Indian companies operating in Liberia, ranging from small trading firms to medium manufacturing enterprises.	SDR 11.15 mn towards the IMF's Financial Package for Liberia's Debt Relief, agricultural assistance package, consisting of pesticides and sprayers	Contribution of a 125-member, Female Formed Police Unit (FFPU) of the CRPF to the United Nations Mission in Liberia since 2007
Libya	Trade of $ 584.58 Million		Projects under Hydrocarbon, Power, Construction and IT sector, BHEL, OVL, IOC, Oil India,			Building hospitals, houses, schools, roads, power plants, airports, dams, transmission lines

Countries	Trade /trade assistance	Training	Projects	Deputation of Indian Experts	Gift & Dona-tions	Capacity Building
Maldives	Trade of US$100 million	Trains at least 200 students a year in various technical/voca-ticnal disciplines,	Projects under Island resorts, export of marine products and busi-ness enterprises.	Doctors, nurses and technicians, teachers, con-struction workers, tailors, etc	US $ 100 million was subscribed to by the State Bank of India ,Tsunami Related Assistance	Taj Group of India runs Taj Exotica Resort & Spa and Vi-vanta Coral Reef Resort in Mal-dives.25 MW wind farm and construction of 500 housing units.
Mali	US$ 15 million for rural electrification, US$ 100 million for financing a power transmission project	30 Seats under ITEC training programme, 8 fel-lowships under CV Raman International Fe lowship pro-gramme.	Projects under automobile sector, ,pharmaceutical products, agro-in-dustries and steel	500 Indians pri-vate Indian busi-nesses in trading jewellery and Iron and Steel		300,000 MTA of steel produc-tion and 70 MW of power generation, oil & gas block for exploration in the Taoudeni basin

Countries	Trade /trade assistance	Training	Projects	Deputation of Indian Experts	Gift & Donations	Capacity Building
Mauritius	Credit line of US $ 250 million and a grant of US$ 20 million	50 Police force are trained, 120 civilian officials are training in Indian institutions and 100 scholarships are given .	Hospital project , Equipment for Eye Hospital, Up gradation of Training Institute, Court House Building, ISRO TTC Station, Science Centre, Cyber Tower and Conference Centre	Visits of Indian Naval Ships to Mauritius	The interceptor patrol boat, CGS Observer to Mauritius on a free lease gifted 2 Chetaks	A Coastal Radar Surveillance System, Supply of an Offshore Patrol boat.

Countries	Trade /trade assistance	Training	Projects	Deputation of Indian Experts	Gift & Donations	Capacity Building
Mongolia	Credit of US $ 20 million	150 Slots under ITEC civilian training programme	Field of geology and mineral resources solar energy electrification project			Setting up a Vocational Training Centre, centre of Excellence (ABVCE) in Information and Communication Technology (ICT) and 5 Community Information Centres (CICs) in 5 provinces were established
Morocco	Bilateral trade US $ 1.2- 1.4 billion		Projects under pharmaceuticals, produce phosphoric acid and Tata Chemicals Limited	Delegations from ASSOCHAM, CAPEXIL and TEXPROCIL,		Tata Motors is producing bus bodies in Casablanca, Tata Consultancy Services (TCS) have set up an off-shoring delivery centre

Countries	Trade /trade assistance	Training	Projects	Deputation of Indian Experts	Gift & Donations	Capacity Building
Myanmar	US$500 million Credit	Training programmes under ITEC, TCS, ICCR – 10 and MGCSS - 10, GCSS and MGCSS schemes.	The Kaladan Multimodal Transport Project ADSL project for high speed data link in 32 Myanmar cities, rail transportation system and in supply of railway coaches.	Export-import business employees and employees of MNC	Reconstruction of 1 high school and 6 primary schools in Tarlay township	Development of 160 km. long Tamu-Kalewa-Kalemyo road, construction of the Rhi-Tiddim Road, Rice Bio Park demonstrating techniques in rice biomass and developing an Information Technology Institute in Mandalay.
Nepal	Assistance of 3600 crores, over 370 projects with an outlay of approx 402 crores.	180 training slots for NA, 1500 scholarships are offered annually for Nepalese students	Projects under infrastructure, health, rural and community development and education.			Helping the Nepal Army (NA) in its modernization through equipment and training.

Countries	Trade /trade assistance	Training	Projects	Deputation of Indian Experts	Gift & Dona-tions	Capacity Building
Niger	Credit of USD 17 million and another of USD 20 million.	Training under Indian Technical & Economic Cooperation (ITEC) and 53 IAFS training slots been given.	Projects under infrastructure, transport, energy, mining, ICT, health and agriculture.	Indian experts in ICT, agriculture sectors Mines and Energy and dry-land agricultural research.	Financial assistance of USD 1,00,000 for food, cash grant of Euro 86,452 and-relief package of basic medicines	
Nigeria	Trade of US$ 13 billion	130 Seat under ITEC	Projects in hydro-carbon and refining	Over 100 Indian companies in pharmaceuticals, steel and power transmission sectors		Development of Mega-Fertilizer Project in Koko Free Trade Zone, Delta

Countries	Trade /trade assistance	Training	Projects	Deputation of Indian Experts	Gift & Dona- tions	Capacity Building
Palestine	Support of US $10 million and an additional $10 million	Eight scholarships ,Special Course for Palestine Diplo- mats (SCPD)and 100slots under ITEC	$10 million in proj- ect assistance for Palestinian development pro- grammes.		US$ 1 million to United Nations Relief and Works Agency (UNRWA)	Library at the Al Azhar University, Library-cum-Stu- dent Activity Centre at the Palestine Techni- cal College an Indoor Multi- purpose Sports Complex has been construct- ed under IBSA
Papua New Guinea	US $ 0.5 million trade assistance	Training of 300 of- ficers/students under ITEC. Also members of the PNG Defence Forc- es were trained.	Projects related to Natural Gas in Southern Highland Province and non- ferrous metals/ores re- sources.	Chartered ac- countants, univer- sity professors, school teachers, doctors, IT and finance professionals	US $ 0.5 million for supply of equipment and material for social and medi- cal programmes, humanitarian aid and disaster relief for natural disasters	Developing 13 vocational train- ing colleges. and infrastructure developments include roads, airports, telecommunica- tions, etc

Countries	Trade /trade assistance	Training	Projects	Deputation of Indian Experts	Gift & Donations	Capacity Building
Republic of Congo	Assistance of USD 70 million	25 Slots under ITEC	Setting up Agricultural Seed Production-cum-Demonstration Centre (ASPDC), India's assistance in economic, scientific and technical fields, infrastructure sector and railways in particular.			Tele-education, tele-medicine and VVIP connectivity node is being set up in Brazzaville under the Pan African e - Network Project. Setting up of a Rural Technology Park (RTP) and a Food Testing Laboratory (FTL).
Rwanda	Credit of US$ 80 million	500 Rwandan students joined Indian universities. ICCR offers six scholarships	Pharmaceuticals, vehicles including motorcycles, plastics and machinery projects.	Forty Indian teachers also joined various institutions in Rwanda, deputation of teachers from (VIT)		Construction of a 27.5 MW hydroelectric project and tele-medicine and tele-education centres in Rwanda

Countries	Trade /trade assistance	Training	Projects	Deputation of Indian Experts	Gift & Donations	Capacity Building
Senegal	Trade of US$425.48 million	45 Slots under ITEC	Industries Chimique du Senegal (ICS) is in the business of manufacturing, supply of buses and spares by Tata International and project to obtain phosphoric acid from the rock phosphate		Jaipur Foot were gifted to around 500 people including soldiers and civilian	Rural electrification and fishing industry development project, acquired railway coaches and locomotives from India. Developed IT Sector, hardware and logistics.
Seychelles	Trade of US$ 28 million	6 Civilians and 33 Defence personnel are trained under ITEC programme	Projects related to Healthcare, Defence and Science and Tech	Deputed six defence officers and one civilian officer.	Gifted a naval patrol vessel 'INS Tarmugli' also books and Pharmaceuticals	Indian Navy is actively engaged in patrolling the Seychelles EEZ against Somalian pirates. Indian Naval ship Sarvekshak conducted hydrographic survey of Aldabra island.

Countries	Trade /trade assistance	Training	Projects	Deputation of Indian Experts	Gift & Donations	Capacity Building
Sierra Leone	Credit (LOC) of US$ 20 million also concessional loans worth US$ 74.45 mn.	25 Slots under ITEC program,	ABG Group discovered significant bauxite deposits, estimated to be 321 mn MT, in 2011.	India's Peacekeeping Role, Feb. 2001, deployed 4000- Indian military contingent in the (UNAMSIL) Maj Gen VK Jetley as Force Commander of UNAMSIL, Indian troops were phased out in January, 2001.	Gifted 200 military barracks to Sierra Leone. Gifted 29 packages of indelible ink, 40,000 tonnes of non-basmati rice.	Expansion of Sierra Leone National Telecommunications Network (SIERRATEL), restoration and rehabilitation of six potable water projects in Freetown.
Somalia	US$ 2 million to the African Union Mission for Somalia (AMISOM).	35 training scholarship	Pan African e-Network project	4,600 Indian peacekeepers, led by Brigadier MP Bhagat, participated in UN-OSOM II, distributed medicines and seeds worth Rs 10 lakh.	US$ 8 million towards humanitarian assistance and donated 100,000 tonnes of wheat.	Indian troops were engaged in reconstruction and humanitarian work, Indian Navy has been involved in anti-piracy patrolling in the Gulf of Aden.

Countries	Trade /trade assistance	Training	Projects	Deputation of Indian Experts	Gift & Donations	Capacity Building
South Sudan		90 ITEC slots under ITEC have been availed	Pan African e-Network Project and in fields of agriculture, horticulture, animal husbandry, rural development, health and education, technical training, HRD and hydrocarbon.			Solar Electrification Project along with construction of (1) a hospital (2) Vocational Training Centre (3) a Rural Technology Park and (4) Agricultural Seed Production and Development Centre in South Sudan.
Suriname	LOC of US $ 10.4 million	25 Training slots to Suriname	Develop a 40,000 hectare palm oil project in Suriname.		Fund and set up an IT Centre in Suriname as a gift.	Setting up of a 161 KV 55 KM long power transmission line Paranam to Paramaribo by PEC and L&T

Countries	Trade /trade assistance	Training	Projects	Deputation of Indian Experts	Gift & Donations	Capacity Building
Syria	Credit line of US$ 100 million		Project on phosphate and fertilizer sector, exploration of oil/natural gas, supply of tractors			India-Syria Centre of Excellence in IT has been set up at Damascus also setting up a Biotechnology Centre
Tanzania	LOC of US$ 40 million for agriculture sector, US$ 180 million for water supply projects	175 trainees are trained annually	A Centre of Excellence in ICT by C-DAC, and the Pan African e-Network Project by TCIL.	28 Indian professors/ lecturers have been deputed to the University of Dodoma. A Delegation from EDCIL, led by CMD, visited Tanzania.	Gifted 5,000 tons each of wheat and rice and ,gifted two raw cashew nut processing plants in Tanzania	L&T constructed a gas processing plant at Songo, NMDC is carrying out gold exploration in Tanzania.

Countries	Trade /trade assistance	Training	Projects	Deputation of Indian Experts	Gift & Donations	Capacity Building
Togo	LOC of US$ 33.04 million &US$ 13 million	Professionals were trained under the capacity building courses conducted by the IIFT	Projects under Health Equipment, farming and cultivation of rice, maize and sorghum in Togo.		Gifted consignment of medicines.	Development of Human Settlement Centre, and India-Africa Centre for English Language Training
Tonga	Aid of US$ 100,000		Project for the jetty reconstruction		Donated 1,200 full uniform sets	Aid of US$ 100,000 for construction of access road from Wharf to Hunga village.
Tunisia	Bilateral trade of US$ 205.95 Million	45 ITEC training slots have been earmarked for Tunisia	Indian joint venture in Tunisia – "Tunisia-India Fertilizer SA" (TIFERT) for manufacturing Phosphoric Acid.			Indian companies are presently engaged in supply and erection of electric transmission lines worth US$ 73 million

Countries	Trade /trade assistance	Training	Projects	Deputation of Indian Experts	Gift & Donations	Capacity Building
Tuvalu	US$ 100,000 million Grant-aid to all Pacific Island	Eight slots under ITEC				Provided computers and medicines & medical equipment for the Princess Margaret Hospital, also supplied two chain-saws.
Uganda	Trade of US$ 678.5 million.	76 slots under ITEC & scholarships are offered by ICCR,	Setting up of a Food Processing Business Incubation Centre and a Tele-medical centre has been set up in Mulago	An Indian Army Training Team (IATT) led by a Brigadier and consisting of two Colonels and one Group Captain is in Uganda		India has offered setting up of three institutions, Institute of Foreign Trade and Food Processing Business Incubation Centre and Material Testing Laboratory

Countries	Trade /trade assistance	Training	Projects	Deputation of Indian Experts	Gift & Donations	Capacity Building
Uruguay	Trade of US$ 80 million	3 ITEC scholarships	Investment in pharma and agri-business sector			TCS has established a Global Delivery IT Centre in Montevideo.
Vanuatu	Trade of US$ 2.43 million	14 Scholars have been trained.				US$ 0.5 million supply of equipment and materials for social and economic programmes and for sustainable development.
Yemen	Grant of US$ 2.3 million	65 Slots under ITEC	Seven oil blocks are being operated by three Indian companies		Food assistance to the tune of Rs 100 million to Yemen through the WFP	Setting up a 200-bed hospital

Countries	Trade /trade assistance	Training	Projects	Deputation of Indian Experts	Gift & Donations	Capacity Building
Zambia	Credit line of $ 10 million	300 Defence officers are being trained	Pre-fabricated health posts in the rural areas of Zambia		Grant of Rs 1 crore for flood relief. Rs 25 million for donation of agricultural equipment	India had deputed, since 1994, a Military Advisory Team which ends its tenure in 2010
Zimbabwe	Bilateral trade of US$125.51 million	150 Trainees trained under ITEC	Projects in Energy and Mining & Construction sectors			

Annexure 3

Government of India
Ministry of External Affairs
Technical Cooperation Division

DEPUTATION OF EXPERT FROM INDIA UNDER THE INDIAN TECHNICAL AND ECONOMIC COOPERATION (ITEC) PROGRAMME

APPLICATION FORM

Name of the host country		
Designation of the proposed Expert		
Period of deputation	From	To
	dd/mm/yy	dd/mm/yy

Part – I

TO BE FILLED BY HOST GOVERNMENT

1	Description of the project.[1]		
2	Aims and objectives to be achieved through the proposed deputation of the Expert		
3	Description of staff to be attached with the Expert on the project.		
4	Place of deployment, address and telephone number.	Place	
		Address	
		Telephone:	
		Fax:	
		Email:	

[1] (Please attach separate sheets if space is not enough; also attach detailed documentation (including statistics) regarding present status and future plans.

Part – II

SPECIFICATIONS FOR THE POST [2]

5.	**Duties of the Expert** (Job description)	
6.	**Educational/Technical** **Qualifications required**	
7.	**Work Experience required**	
8.	**Field of Specialization –** (Type of material, equipment and machinery etc. with which the Expert is expected to be familiar)	

2 [Please attach separate sheet(s), if space is not enough in these columns]

Part – III

UNDERTAKING TO BE GIVEN BY THE HOST GOVERNMENT

The Host Government hereby undertakes:

- To provide furnished accommodation suitable for the Expert and members of his family;

- To pay subsistence allowance to the Expert while on internal tour away from Headquarters;

- To incur expenditure on internal travel or provide transport to the Expert on official tour/duty;

- To grant leave to the Expert as admissible;

- To extend free hospital and medical treatment to the Expert and members of his family;

- To exempt the Expert and members of his family from payment of customs duty on their personal effects when imported on first arrival within reasonable period;

- To exempt the Expert from paying income-tax;

- To indemnify the Expert in respect of damages suffered/ awarded against him for actions performed in the course of official duty; and

- If extension of deputation period by any time exceeding three months was sought by the host Government, the cost of terminal passage, transportation of baggage, Children Holiday Passage (restricted to two children) and return Home Leave Fares of expert and entitled members of his family would be borne by the host Government.

Date :

Place :   Authorized Signatory
                                                          Seal

Part – IV

CERTIFICATE TO BE GIVEN BY THE INDIAN MISSION

1. The ITEC Expert form has been personally scrutinized by the officer-in-charge of ITEC work in consultation with HOM.

2. The Form is complete [in triplicate] in respect of answers to all questions and is accompanied by required documentation and details of the project for which the Expert is required.

3. The deputation of the Expert is required for the exact period of days/ months/years. The period of deputation has been discussed with the host Government which considers it adequate and no extension would be necessary.

4. A note has been attached containing details of exact location of the place of Expert's deployment, its distance from the capital city, climate conditions, requirement of dress and clothing, level of educational facilities available for Expert's children (including medium of instructions), hospital and medical facilities available, availability of food items locally and to be brought from India, currency and its exchange rate, mode of payment to the Expert and remittance facility to India.

5. The host Government has been apprised of the terms and conditions, and have agreed to provide the requisite facilities to the Expert as per Part III of the form.

6. The host Government will provide secretarial assistance to the Expert, where required.

7. A note on assessment of expected benefits to the host Government.

8. The proposed deputation does/does not form part of Joint Commission meeting held on _____ / agreement signed on _____ .

Signature and Seal of
Officer-in-charge of ITEC
in the Mission
Telephone No :
(Off.)
(Res.)

Remarks/Recommendations
of HOM/HOP.

Signature

Date :   (Seal – HOM/HOP)

DEPUTATION OF INDIAN EXPERT ABROAD –

GUIDELINES FOR SUBMISSION OF FORM

- The Form, in triplicate, are required to be submitted to Technical Cooperation Division of Ministry of External Affairs, New Delhi.

- All the columns in the Form are required to be filled in and signed by the Authorized Signatory with seal, wherever required, and submitted with necessary documentations. Incomplete Form will not be entertained.

- Each request for deputation of expert is required to be submitted in separate Form.

- The host Government is required to furnish in detail the "Specifications for the Post' in Part-II of the Form and also specify the period of deputation.

- The Indian Mission is required to apprise the host Government about the terms and conditions of the deputation of Expert.

GOVERNMENT OF INDIA   Annexure 4

MINISTRY OF EXTERNAL AFFAIRS
INDIAN TECHNICAL AND ECONOMIC COOPERATION (ITEC) AND
SPECIAL COMMONWEALTH ASSISTANCE FOR AFRICA PROGRAMME (SCAAP)
(Application for the courses fully funded by the Ministry of External Affairs,
Government of India)

Please read instructions carefully before applying

APPLICATION FORM

3 X 4 cm

PART- I

Nationality: _____ Name of Course: _____
Institute : _____ Commencing :
                              From _____ to _____
                              DD/MM/YYYY   DD/MM/YYYY

1. Personal Particulars
Name(s): _____
Surname: _____
Sex (tick one): MALE / FEMALE
Marital Status: _____
Date of Birth: _____
                    Date - Month - Year

Passport No.:- _____Date & Place of Issue :- _____Valid till :- _____

Address:	Office	Res.
Tel Nos.		
Mobile/Cell:		
Fax:		
E-mail:		
Special dietary needs if any: _____		

Person(s) to be notified in case of Emergency

	Official Contact	Personal / Family Contact
Name : Address: Tel Nos: Mobile/Cell Fax: E-mail		

Educational Qualification/(s)

Degree / Diploma / Certificates	Year	Name of Educational Institute
1.		
2.		
3.		
4.		

Professional Qualification(s), if any:

Professional Qualification (s)	Year	Name of Institute
1.		
2.		
3.		
4.		

2. Details of Employment/Profession (current & previous)

Name of Employer / Department / Company	Position	Period	Description of Work

Are you an employee of: (Mark appropriate box)

a. Government ☐   b. Semi-government/Parastatal . ☐

c. Private Company ☐   d. Self -employed ☐   e. Others . ☐

Details of present employer :

Name / address_____

Tel No:_____

E-mail:

3. Have you ever attended a course sponsored by the Government of India? (Mark one)

| YES | NO |

(i) If answer to 3 is yes, details of the Course _____

4. Details of Course(s) attended, if any, outside your country:

Country	Course Details & Duration	Year	Sponsor / Programme

5. Please describe in your own words (about 100 words):

(a) qualification/experience in the related to the course applied for; &

(b) reason (s) for applying for this training course.

6. Certification of English language proficiency (by Indian Mission/Designated Authority)

	Good	Basic	Remarks
Spoken			
Written			

Mother tongue / Native language:_____/ Other language(s), if any:

_____

English Language test administered by:	_____

Name & Address:_____   Tel No:_____

_____   E-mail:_____

_____   Signature with date

MEDICAL REPORT

(To be certified by a doctor/hospital on the panel of the Indian Mission, UN Mission, if any or as designated by Indian Mission)

(i) Name of Applicant	
(ii) Age:	
(iii) Sex: (Male/ Female)	
(iv) Height (cm)	
(v) Weight (kg)	
(vi) Blood Group	
(vii) Blood Pressure	

1. Is the person examined in good health at present	
2. Is the person examined physically and mentally able to carry out intensive training away from home?	
3. Is the person free of infectious diseases (HIV/AIDS, tuberculosis, trachoma, skin diseases etc), Yellow fever certificate (in case of people coming from that region or as laid out in WHO Regulations).	
4. Does the person examined has any medical condition or defect which might require treatment during the course ?	
5. List of any observed abnormalities indicated in the chest X ray.	

I certify that the applicant is medically fit to undertake a training course in India.

Name of Doctor/Physician: _____

Registration No.: _____

Address of Clinic / Hospital _____

and City / Town : _____

Telephone : _____

E mail: _____ Date: _____

Signature of Doctor/Physician: _____ Seal of Clinic/Hospital: _____

IMPORTANT NOTICE

- Please read the form carefully. The application will be automatically rejected if any column is inaccurate, incomplete or blank.

- Declaration by the candidate and the recommendations from employer, if any, are compulsory pre- requisites.

- Working knowledge of the English language is a pre-requisite. For English language and language related courses, basic knowledge of English is required.

- Candidates who leave the course midway for personal reasons without prior permission of the Ministry of External Affairs or remain absent from the programme without sufficient reasons are expected to refund the cost of training and airfare to Government of India.

- Female candidates are hereby advised that they should not travel to India to attend the course applied for in case they are in family way.

UNDERTAKING BY THE APPLICANT

I, _____

(Name, Middle name, Family name)

of (country)_____ certify that information provided by me in this form is true, complete and correct.

I also certify that :-

(i) I have read the course brochure and that I am aware of the course contents and living conditions in India *.

(ii) I have sufficient knowledge of English to participate in the training programme.

(iii) I am medically fit to participate in the Course and have submitted a medical certificate from the designated doctor.

(iv) I have not attended any programme previously sponsored by Government of India.

(v) I have not applied for or am not required to attend any other training course/conference/meeting etc. during the period of the course applied for.

If accepted for the ITEC / SCAAP training programme, I undertake to:

- (a) Comply with the instructions and abide by Rules, Regulations and guidelines as may be stipulated by both the nominating and sponsoring Governments in respect of the training;

- (b) Follow the full and complete course of study or training and abide by the Rules of the University/Institution/ Establishment in which I undertake to study or undergo training;

- (c) Submit periodic assessments / tests conducted by the Institute (progress report which may be prescribed);

- (d) Refrain from engaging in political activity, or any form of employment for profit or gain;

- (e) Return to my home country at the end of the course of study or training;

- (f) I also fully undertake that if I am granted a training award, it may be subsequently withdrawn if I fail to make adequate progress or for other sufficient cause determined by the host Government.

For lady participants :- I confirm that I will not travel to India to attend the Course I have applied for if I am in the family way.

Date:

Place:

(SIGNATURE OF THE APPLICANT)

Name: _____

*Details of the course are on the website of the Institute or can be obtained from them by e-mail.

PART – II

To be completed by the authorized official of the

Nominating Government/Employer

I, _____ on behalf of the Government of_____ certify that:

(a) I have examined the educational, professional and other certificates quoted by the nominee in Part – I of this form and I am satisfied that they are authentic and relate to the nominee.

(b) I have gone through the medical certificates and X-ray reports produced by the nominee which state that he/she is medically fit and free from any infectious disease such as HIV/AIDS and Yellow Fever and that having regard to his/her physical and mental history there is no reason to indicate that the nominee is other than fit to undertake the journey to India and to undergo training in India.

(c) The nominee has adequate knowledge of spoken and written English to enable him to follow the course of training for which he/she is being nominated.

(d) The nominee has not availed of ITEC/SCAAP training facilities earlier in India.

I nominate Mr./Mrs./Miss_____on behalf of the Government of_____/as employer.

Name of Nominating Authority:
Designation:
Address:
Date:
Place:

Signature
(With seal)

Name and Designation

(in block letters)

Annexure 5

MEMORANDUM OF UNDERSTANDING
Between
THE UNITED NATIONS
And
THE ELECTION COMMISSION OF INDIA
for
COOPERATION IN ELECTORAL ASSISTANCE

The United Nations and The Election Commission of India, hereinafter the "Parties",

Recalling the principles of the United Nations General Assembly resolution 46/137 of 17 December 1991, to enhance the effectiveness of periodic and genuine elections;

Considering that said resolution requested, *inter alia*, the Secretary-General of the United Nations to ensure consistency in the handling of requests of Member States organizing elections, to coordinate and consider requests for electoral verification and to channel requests for electoral assistance to the appropriate office or programme, to build on experience gained to develop an institutional memory, to develop and maintain a roster of international experts who could provide technical assistance and to maintain contact with regional and other intergovernmental organizations to ensure appropriate working arrangements with them;

Recognizing the need to establish a mechanism for cooperation in the design and implementation of the electoral process; and for exchange, consultation and cooperation in programmes and activities in the field of electoral administration;

Hereby agree as follows :

ARTICLE I

The Parties undertake to promote cooperation, on mutually agreed terms & conditions in priority areas in the field of electoral assistance, including:

(a) Promotion of initiatives designed to strengthen electoral systems and democratic institutions;

(b) Promotion of exchanges of knowledge and experience in the field of organizational and technical development, with a view to strengthening the administration of electoral processes;

(c) In providing assistance to Member States' electoral authorities in the organization and conduct of electoral processes on demand;

(d) Enhancing the coordination of activities and the exchange of experts with other national electoral authorities, intergovernmental, nongovernmental or other international entities;

(e) Nomination of the Election Commission of India personnel for inclusion into the United Nations electoral experts roster;

(f) Provision of personnel, logistical and technical assistance to United Nations electoral observation and monitoring activities;

(g) Facilitating relationships with other national electoral authorities;

(h) Production and dissemination of materials pertaining to electoral systems, voting technology, processes or related areas ; and

(i) Any other modality of cooperation mutually agreed on by the Parties.

ARTICLE II

With a view to maintaining an appropriate mechanism for implementation of and follow-up to this Memorandum, the parties shall conduct periodic consultations for the purpose of:

(a) Identifying and evaluating priority areas for carrying out specific technical cooperation activities;

(b) Recommending and preparing instruments designed to identify activities, programmes and projects to be executed, as well as assessing their implementation;

(c) overseeing proper observance of and compliance with this Memorandum;

ARTICLE III

Nothing in this memorandum shall, in any way, prevent either Party from entering into bilateral agreements with other countries on matters covered under this MoU.

ARTICLE IV

In the implementation of this Memorandum, the parties shall conclude Project Documents for technical cooperation, setting out the terms and conditions of such cooperation, the financial resources required and the legal status of the personnel involved. Other forms of cooperation under this Memorandum will be implemented through existing legal and administrative arrangements.

ARTICLE V

Any dispute between the Parties relating to the jnterpretation and application of this Memorandum shall be settled by negotiations or other mutually agreed mode of settlement.

ARTICLE VI

This Memorandum may be amended by written agreement between the parties.

ARTICLE VII

This Memorandum shall enter into force on the date of its signature and shall remain in force until terminated by either Party upon written notice and the orderly cessation of on-going technical cooperation activities.

Signed in the city of New Delhi, India on the twenty eighth day of the month of August in the year two thousand and four, in two originals in English language, each text being equally authentic.

For the Election Commission of India	For the United Nations
Dr. NOOR MOHAMMAD DEPUTY ELECTION COMMISSIONER ELECTION COMMISSION OF INDIA	CARINA PERELLI DIRECTOR ELECTORAL ASSISTANCE DIVISION DEPARTMENT OF POLITICAL AFFAIRS UNITED NATIONS

Annexure 6

CIVILIAN CAPACITY: ENHANCING THE DEPLOYMENT OF RULE OF LAW EXPERTS

Introduction

The word 'peacekeeping' has been employed to include a large number of military and related activities involving the use of force in self-defence or the immediate defence of non-combatants, for observing ceasefire and force separation to bring peace in conflict ridden state(s). The key objective of peacekeeping has been to help preserve the international state system. The post-conflict peace-building (PCPB) measures initiated by the United Nations (UN) and some of its Member-States in conflict-ridden societies have been unsuccessful in the recent past. With the dominance of military personnel, the approach has remained confined to demobilization, disarmament and re-integration of former combatants. In fact, the potential of the UN to adopt an integrated approach to peace-building has not been fully developed, by either the UN or its agencies and the deployment of civilians in international peace operations has remained a marginal issue.

The Brahimi Report (2000) brought out certain shortcomings in the peacekeeping system. This has resulted in a qualitative transformation in peacekeeping efforts, and the proportion of civilians in multi-dimensional missions is increasing. For instance, as on 28 February 2013, nearly 5100 international civilians were serving in peacekeeping operations worldwide. However, one of the persistent criticisms levelled against the existing system is that a group of developed states has been 'ganging-up' for top positions, with the domestic actors being forced to make do with positions pre-agreed among the external actors. Such an approach does not encourage local ownership and the contextualization of responses to the local needs, priorities and socio-cultural environment, and thus leads to failure of the PCPB missions.

UN: Civilian Capacities

The Brahimi Report also called upon Member States to establish enhanced national 'pools' of police officers and related experts, to be drawn upon for deployment to UN operations, to help meet the high demand for civilian police and related criminal justice/rule of law experts in peace operations dealing with intra-State conflict. A few changes that the Brahimi Panel supported were: "a doctrinal shift in the use of civilian police and related rule of law elements in peace operations that emphasizes a team approach to upholding the rule of law and respect for human rights and helping communities coming out of a conflict to achieve national reconciliation;..... make a real difference in the lives of people in the mission area; and better integration of electoral assistance into a broader strategy for the support of governance institutions." [1]

There has been a shift in the UN approach from military to civilian-oriented peace missions as the mandate has shifted from monitoring military ceasefires to supporting the implementation of comprehensive peace agreements. The role of civilians has become more central, to peace-building missions. Not only has the number of civilian functions increased, civilians have also shifted from a peripheral support role to the core of contemporary PKPB missions. They now constitute 14.9% of all UN peacekeepers and peace-builders. As on 28 February 2013, the UN had deployed 16,831 civilians, including 5,107 international staff, and 11,724 local staff.[2] However, this number is considered grossly inadequate by the UN, as the requirement has steadily increased over the years.

Despite the fact that a great number of people are eager to serve in UN missions, the civilian vacancy rates in UN missions is high. Under the existing system, applicants across the world apply directly to the UN. The ensuing process of screening and

---

1   See UN document: A/55/305–S/2000/809 dated 21 August 2000.

2   http://www.un.org/en/peacekeeping/resources/statistics/factsheet.shtml

recruitment may take approximately 200 days. Clearly, the system is too slow and bureaucratic to meet the deployment needs of the PKPB missions.[3] One of the problems faced by those responsible for recruitments seems to be the quality and appropriateness of the candidates who are short-listed for selection. Though one may grant that it is difficult to find candidates to fill vacancies in certain specialized categories, including security sector reform, and judicial and prison management, an assumption that there is a worldwide shortage of civilian expertise appears flawed.

In order to meet the requirement of civilian capacities, the UN needs to: (i) decentralize the system of civilian capacities selection, (ii) allocate the vacancies and the expertise need to the Member States as in the case of military/police personnel, (iii) identify training needs in each category of civilian capacity, and (iv) allocate funds for their training.

Rule of Law[4]

The basic principle on which the Rule of Law rests is: "No one is above the law." The rule follows logically from the idea that truth, and therefore law, is based upon fundamental principles which can be discovered, but which cannot be created through an act of will. It is based on the ideas of freedom, justice, human rights and liberties of individuals not only against their fellow men but also

---

3   Solli, A., de Carvalho, B., de Coning, C.H. and Pedersen, M.F. 2009, *Bottlenecks to Deployment: The Challenges of Deploying Civilian Personnel to Peace Operations*, Security in Practice 3/2009, Oslo: Norwegian Institute of International Affairs, p.10.

4   The UN Rule of Law Indicators were endorsed, through the Rule of Law Coordination and Resource Group, by the Department of Political Affairs and the Office of Legal Affairs of the United Nations, the United Nations Children's Fund, the United Nations Development Programme, the United Nations Entity for Gender Equality and the Empowerment of Women (UN-Women), the Office of the United Nations High Commissioner for Refugees and the United Nations Office on Drugs and Crime. All the members of the Rule of Law Coordination and Resource Group and the World Bank provided advice and support. The UN Rule of Law Indicators were developed with the assistance of the Vera Institute of Justice / Altus Global Alliance (VIJ/AGA), a network of six nongovernmental organizations and academic centres based in Brazil, Chile, India, Nigeria, Russia, and the United States, and consultants from the University of the Fraser Valley and Harvard University. This instrument was tested on a pilot basis in Haiti and Liberia.

against arbitrary governance. Today, the importance of the rule of law is unquestionable. It has been recognized in the Universal Declaration of Human Rights of 1948, which states that "... it is essential, if man is not to be compelled to have recourse, as a last resort, to rebellion against tyranny and oppression, that human rights should be protected by the Rule of Law...."[5]

The Indian Constitution

The doctrine of Rule of Law has been adopted in the Indian Constitution. The ideals of the Constitution: justice, liberty and equality are enshrined in the preamble. The Constitution has been made the supreme law of the country and other laws are required to be in conformity with it. It not only lays down the framework of the Indian judicial system, but has also the powers, duties, procedures and structure of the various branches of the government at the Union and State levels. It also defines the rights and duties of the people and the directive principles that are to guide the State in the future. Part III of the Constitution guarantees the Fundamental Rights. Article 13(I) makes it clear that all laws in force in the territory of India immediately before the commencement of the Constitution, in so far as they are inconsistent with the provisions of Part III shall, to the extent of such inconsistency, be void. Article 13(2) provides that the State should not make any law which takes away or abridges the Fundamental Rights and that any law made in contravention of this clause shall, to the extent of the contravention, be void.

The Constitution guarantees equality before the law and equal protection of laws. Article 21 guarantees right to life and personal liberty. It provides that no person shall be deprived of his life or personal liberty except according to the procedure established by law. Article 19 guarantees six Fundamental Freedoms to the citizens of India -- freedom of speech and expression, freedom of assembly, freedom to form associations or unions, freedom to live in any part of the territory of India and freedom of profession, occupation,

---

5   Preamble, Universal Declaration of Human Rights, 1948.

trade or business. The right to these freedoms is not absolute, but subject to the reasonable restrictions which may be imposed by the State. Article 20(1) provides that no person shall be convicted of any offence except for violation of a law in force at the time of the commission of the act charged as an offence and not be subject to a penalty greater than that which might have been inflicted at the time of the commission of the offence. According to Article 20(2), no person shall be prosecuted and punished for the same offence more than once. Article 20(3) makes it clear that no person accused of an offence shall be compelled to be witness against himself.

The Constitution is supreme and the three organs of the government viz. legislature, executive and judiciary are subordinate to it. The legislature or the Indian Parliament consists of two houses, the Lok Sabha and the Rajya Sabha. The executive comprises the President and the council of ministers headed by the Prime Minister. The judiciary, which is the custodian of the Fundamental Rights, is headed by the Chief Justice of India. While the legislature lays down the law and the executive implements it, the judiciary determines whether the action taken by the executive is in accordance with the law and may question the constitutional validity of a law.

India strongly supports adherence to the rule of law both at the national and international levels. In India, the promotion of the rule of law is an essential tool for ensuring sustainable development and peaceful coexistence and cooperation among States. Article 51 of the Indian Constitution states: "The State shall endeavour to promote international peace and security; and foster respect for international law and treaty obligations in the dealings of organized people with one another."

Rule of Law Experts

India stands solidly committed to assisting the UN in the maintenance of international peace and security. We have a proud history of UN peacekeeping dating back to its inception in the 1950s. We have contributed nearly 160,000 troops, and participated in 43 missions. India has also provided and continues to provide eminent Force

Commanders for UN Missions. Indian troops have taken part in some of the most difficult operations, and their professional excellence has won them universal admiration.

Besides, the civilian expertise available in India is capable of strengthening the rule of law during PCPB efforts through legislative and judicial reforms; training of the local police and restructuring of the penal system; improving respect for human rights through monitoring, education and investigation of past and existing abuses; providing assistance for democratic processes, for example, electoral assistance; reforming the military justice system; and promoting conflict resolution.

Some of the ministries and institutions that have such expertise are as follows.

Ministry of Law and Justice. The Ministry of Law and Justice is the oldest limb of the Government of India, dating back to 1833 when the Charter Act 1833 was enacted by the British Parliament. It advises the other departments and ministries on legal matters, including interpretation of the Constitution and laws, conveyancing and engagement of counsels to appear on behalf of the Union of India in the High Courts and subordinate courts where the Union of India is a party. It also advises the government on the conduct of cases in the Supreme Court and the High Courts on behalf of the Union government and the state governments. Its other major function is to make reciprocal arrangements with foreign countries for the service of summons in civil suits, for the execution of decrees of civil courts, for the enforcement of maintenance orders, and for the administration of the estates of foreigners dying in India intestate. The functions of the ministry are distributed between two main departments: (i) the Legislative Department and (ii) the Justice Department.

The Legislative Department deals with the drafting of bills; drafting and promulgation of ordinances and regulations; drafting of constitution orders and notifications for bringing into force constitution (amendment) acts. It has expertise in the preparation and publication of standard legal terminology for use, as far as possible, in all official languages. It also undertakes the task of preparing authoritative texts, in the official languages, of all Central acts and of ordinances promulgated and regulations made by the President. The Justice Department deals with the appointment, resignation and removal of the Chief Justice of India, judges of the Supreme Court, and the Chief Justice and judges of the High Courts. It is also concerned with their salaries, rights in respect of leave of absence (including leave allowances), pensions and travelling allowances. In addition, it has the task of administration of justice and constitution and organization of courts in India. The ministry has a large pool of officers, selected under the Indian Legal Service, who are capable of bringing about reforms in related fields of expertise.

Ministry of Social Justice. The Government of India is a party to (i) the Proclamation on the Full Participation and Equality of People with Disabilities in the Asia-Pacific Region, adopted in Beijing in December 1992, and (ii) The UN Convention on the Rights of Persons with Disabilities (UNCRPD), which came into effect in May 2008. The Ministry of Social Justice & Empowerment was created in 1998 and looks after the welfare of the disabled in India. It runs seven national institutes dealing with various types of disabilities and seven composite regional centres, which provide rehabilitation services to PwDs and run courses for the rehabilitation of professionals. It also funds a large number of NGOs for similar services. The National Handicapped Finance & Development Corporation (NHFDC), which is managed by the ministry, provides loans at concessional rates for self-employment. The ministry has a large pool of experts who are capable of dealing with issues of social justice and empowerment of the disabled and weaker sections of a society in a post-conflict situation.

Law Commission of India. In the ancient period, when the country was guided by religious and customary law, the process of reform process was ad hoc and not institutionalized through duly constituted law reform agencies. However, since the third decade of the nineteenth century, Law Commissions were constituted from time to time to recommend legislative reforms with a view to clarify, consolidate and codify particular branches of law. Some of the products of our first four Law Commissions are the Indian Code of Civil Procedure, the Indian Contract Act, the Indian Evidence Act, and the Transfer of Property Act.

The First Law Commission of Independent India was established in 1955. Law Commissions have the mandate to identify laws which (i) are no longer needed or relevant and can be immediately repealed, (ii) are not in harmony with the existing climate of economic liberalization and need change, and (iii) require changes or amendments and to make suggestions for such amendments. They are also entrusted with the task of suggesting suitable measures for the quick redressal of citizen's grievances in the field of law. They examine laws which affect the poor and carry out post-audits for socio-economic legislations. They take all such measures as may be necessary to harness the legal process for the service of the poor. The Law Commission holds expertise in evaluating and suggesting reforms in the legal system prevailing in any country.

Election Commission. The Election Commission of India (ECI) has emerged, as one of the most respected institutions in the world and its expertise has been sought by a number of countries.[6] The ECI has resources that include knowledge, skills, expertise and experience in terms of election management and related operations for which there is an ever-expanding global demand. With 60 years of experience in the management of the largest and the most complex elections in the world, and with a high degree of efficiency and credibility by global recognition, the ECI has justifiably been requested to share its expertise and skills by several countries. The Commission has responded positively to these requests.

---

6   In India, any voluntary interference or attempt at interfering with the free exercise of any electoral rights constitutes the crime of undue influence at an election under section 171C of the Indian Penal Code. Section 123 of the Representation of Peoples Act 1951 defines any direct or indirect interference with the free exercise of any electoral right as a corrupt practice in India.

The ECIs international engagements include: signing MoUs for cooperation in electoral management with 14 countries, the UNDP; participating in 10 election observation assignments on invitation and receiving representatives of other countries to witness Indian elections; being a member of and on the Steering Committee of the Commonwealth Electoral Network; being founder-member and the current vice-chair of the Association of Asian Election Authorities; and being special invitee to the highly integrated ASEAN forum of Election Management Bodies. The India International Institute of Democracy and Election Management (IIIDEM), which is the training arm of the ECI's institutionalized international cooperation, has held courses for officials from Kenya, Nigeria, the Maldives, Afghanistan, Nepal and Bhutan.

Judicial System. The Indian Judicial System is one of the oldest in the world. The framework of the current system was laid down by the Indian Constitution from which the judicial system derives its powers. Though India has adopted several features of a federal system of government, the Constitution has provided for the setting up of a single integrated system of courts to administer both Union and state laws. The Supreme Court is the apex court, under which are the various high courts, which cater to one or more states. Below the high courts, are the subordinate courts including district courts and lower courts.

The Indian Judicial System is a 'common law system', in which law is developed by the judges through their decisions, orders and judgments. These are also referred to as precedents. Unlike the British legal system, however, the Indian system is not entirely based on common law. It is also based on statutory law and the regulatory law. Much like other common law systems, India follows the adversarial system of conducting proceedings, rather than the inquisitorial system. In an adversarial system, there are two sides in every case and each side presents its arguments to a neutral judge who then passes an order or a judgment based upon the merits of the case.

The Indian judicial system has adopted features of other legal systems in such a way that they do not conflict with each other while benefitting the nation and the people. For example, the Supreme Court and the high courts have the power of judicial review. This is a concept prevalent in the American legal system. According to the concept of judicial review, legislative and executive actions are subject to the scrutiny of the judiciary and the judiciary can invalidate such actions if they are ultra vires of Constitutional provisions.

The district courts in a state are above all the subordinate or lower courts, but under the administrative control of the high court of the state to which they belong. Their jurisdiction is confined to the districts they are responsible for, which could be one or more than one. The original jurisdiction of the district courts in civil matters is confined not only to a certain territorial area, but also to a pecuniary limit. The pecuniary limits are laid down by the legislature and if the amount in dispute is way above the pecuniary jurisdiction of the district court then the matter will be heard by the concerned high court. In the case of criminal matters, the jurisdiction of the courts is laid down by the legislature. The decisions of the district courts are subject to the appellate jurisdiction of the high courts.

Apart from these judicial bodies, there are numerous quasi-judicial bodies that are involved in dispute resolution. These tribunals are constituted as per the relevant statutory provisions and are seen as an alternative forum for the speedy disposal of redressal of grievances and adjudication of disputes. Some important tribunals are the Central Administrative Tribunal, the Telecom Disputes Settlement Appellate Tribunal, the Competition Appellate Tribunal, the Armed Forces Tribunal and the Debt Recovery Tribunal. The kinds of cases the tribunals hear are limited to their specific area.

Police System. The Indian police constitute the primary organ of the administration for ensuring equality before the law and equal protection of the laws. They have served the democratic system by maintaining law and order, prosecuting criminals, seeing to their rehabilitation, conducting fair and efficient elections and fighting terrorism. The first all- women contingent in any UN peacekeeping mission, a Formed Police Unit from India, was deployed in 2007 to the UN Operation in Liberia. These women peacekeepers set an example in preventing violence against women and girls that is now emulated in UN peacekeeping missions across the world. The deployment was hailed as potentially transformative and was seen as a key step towards altering the conditions for local girls and women in post-conflict situations, particularly in the light of increasing reports of sexual exploitation and abuse by male peacekeepers.

Attorney General. The Attorney-General of India is appointed by the President under Article 76 of the Constitution. He renders advice to the Government of India upon such legal matters and to perform such other duties of a legal character as may from time to time be referred or assigned to him by the President. He also discharges the functions conferred on him by or under the Constitution or any other law that is in force for the time being. A large number of qualified law officers with expertise on judicial matters serve under him.

Judge Advocate General. The Judge Advocate Generals (JAG) of the three services of the Indian Armed Forces also have a number of law officers, who, besides being trained in the law of the land, also have expertise in the military law of India. The JAG is the chief law officer and provides expert advice to the Chief of Staff of the service concerned on international, national and military law.

Institutions and Organisations. Several institutions and organizations are associated on a regular basis in the effort to improve the effectiveness of the legal system in the country. They also assist the state and Union governments in building capacity for the promotion of the rule of law at the national and international levels. The United Services Institution of India, Delhi, is one such institution. It is engaged in creating awareness on the rule of law by the dissemination of material and training of civilians, police and military personnel. It also conducts regular training programmes for researchers, students, military personnel and members of the civil society of various countries, in association with the United Nations Institute for Training and Research (UNITAR). The Indian Society of International Law, New Delhi, is dedicated to the development and implementation of international law and principles that advance human rights through the rule of law. It provides legal expertise at the international and national levels. The Supreme Court Bar Association influences the development of international law reform and shapes the future of the legal profession in the country. It also provides voluntary legal service by skilled and experienced lawyers to help governments and citizens develop and implement legal reforms, assist programmes that advance social well-being, and build the capacity of organizations and professionals to meet the needs of their communities.

Rule of Law and Protection and Preservation of Environment

This is a new area on which I would like the UN to focus. The application of the rule of law to the environment could provide an effective mechanism for the peaceful management and settlement of conflicts; protection, preservation and restoration of the natural environment; and prevention of conflicts. Take for instance, the damage to the natural environment of Afghanistan in three decades of conflict. Up to 80 per cent of Afghans depend directly on natural resources, including the 60 percent that depends on agriculture. The combination of intermittent water supply and water contamination has led to over 2.5 million Afghans being affected by drought and water shortages. The situation has made certain sections of the society like minorities, women, children, displaced persons and refugees more vulnerable. The environmental destruction in Afghanistan has been caused by the armed conflict resulting in the collapse of institutions and subsequent decline in the rule of law and the environmental management capacity of communities and the state.

The canvass of the rule of law is expanding. A high-level meeting on the rule of law and the environment took place on

17 February 2013 at the UN Office in Nairobi, Kenya.[7] The aim of the meeting was to provide a platform for participants to discuss important recent developments and new opportunities regarding the rule of law in the field of the environment; and consider how the rule of law can be promoted for greater effect in the quest for environmental sustainability, sustainable development and social justice.

Many countries have taken an initiative to promote environmental conservation. For instance, the Icelandic Constitution drafted in 2012, states: "All shall by law be accorded the right to a healthy environment, fresh water, unpolluted air and unspoiled nature. This means that the diversity of life and land must be maintained and nature's objects of value, uninhabited areas, vegetation and soil shall enjoy protection." This new approach recognizes that the maintenance of life systems, ecological diversity (without genetic alteration), clean water and air, interdependence of the components of nature need legal protection. The rule of law must cover environmental protection to ensure justice and rebuild peace in post-conflict societies.

The expertise of the Indian Ministry of Environment & Forests could be utilized for the promotion and implementation of the environmental policies of the United Nations Environment Programme (UNEP) in PCPB missions. The primary concerns of the Ministry are the implementation of policies and programmes relating to the conservation of the country's natural resources, including lakes rivers and wetlands, and forests and wildlife; the protection of its biodiversity, and the prevention and abatement of pollution. While implementing these policies and programmes, the Ministry is guided by the principle of sustainable development and enhancement of human well-being. The Ministry also serves as the nodal agency in the country for the UNEP, South Asia Cooperative Environment Programme, International Centre for Integrated

---

7   The meeting, which was held on the eve of the 27th session of the Governing Council/Global Ministerial Environment Forum (GC27/GMEF) of the UN Environment Programme (UNEP) was attended by high-ranking representatives of the judicial, legal and auditing professions, among others.

Mountain Development and for the follow-up of the United Nations Conference on Environment and Development. The Ministry is also entrusted with issues relating to multilateral bodies such as the Commission on Sustainable Development, Global Environment Facility and of regional bodies like Economic and Social Council for Asia and Pacific and South Asian Association for Regional Cooperation on matters pertaining to the environment.

Conclusion

Since the Brahimi Report was submitted 13 years ago, considerable civilian capacities have been created worldwide. But progress has been quite uneven across countries and continents. Only a limited number of countries have developed approaches that make use of their own civilian professionals and are compatible with the needs and workflows of the international organizations. It is not a misconception that the Global South is under-represented in civilian posts within UN PCPB missions. For PCPB efforts to be successful, certain gaps need to be addressed. India has a reservoir of motivated and qualified civilians in the field of rule of law. These experts in the fields of legislation, prison reforms, judiciary, prosecution, justice delivery system, public administration, protection of women and children, policy formulation for the poor and disabled, and international humanitarian law and military law can help to broaden the pool of civilian experts needed to support the immediate capacity development of countries emerging from conflict.

Annexure 7

ECOLOGICAL WARRIORS

Introduction

India is fast developing in industrial, social and technological spheres. There are large infrastructural requirements to meet the growing needs. Due to sudden acceleration in growth of industry; pressure on agriculture land, water resources and forests is unprecedented. The ill effects of this enormous growth in terms of ecological degradation were foreseen and vividly read by Dr Norman Borlaugh who suggested to the then Prime Minister, Mrs Indira Gandhi to address this menace on a war footing by involving the Army. Mrs Indira Gandhi and Mr M Swaminathan understood the gravity of situation and cleared the proposal of raising Ecological Battalions in the Country by involving army. This resulted in raising of first Ecological Battalion at Dehradun with the primary aim of greening and rehabilitating over-mined Mussorie hills

The Ecological Battalions of TA are one of its kinds in the world. These battalions are also commonly called as Ecological Task Forces (ETF). The responsibility of greening India has been entrusted to these battalions who take up projects for various States and complete them in a time bound manner. The enrolment in ETFs is based on Ex-servicemen of respective States who after going on discharge from active service are still physically fit to undertake afforestation and other ecological tasks.

Objective

The objective of raising ETFs is to undertake speedy restoration of identified degraded areas, particularly those that are in inhospitable and difficult terrain. The local ex-servicemen are the torch bearers of these Task Forces. This initiative, besides serving the cause of environment restoration, also provides an opportunity for rehabilitation of ex-servicemen. The activities undertaken by

ETFs include afforestation, soil and water conservation, pasture development and other restorative works. The disciplined force of ex-servicemen working on the ethos of armed forces is the ideal force for this sensitive task of ecological conservation. These able bodied soldiers who are used to work as teams are more suited to work in difficult areas like mountain slopes and deserts.

There are eight ETFs working in the Country in five States. These States are; Assam, Delhi, Himachal Pradesh, J&K, Rajasthan and Uttarakhand. These ETF units though raised under Ministry of Defence (MoD), are paid for and funded by Ministry of Environment and Forests (MoEF). There are only two units, one each in Delhi and Himachal Pradesh, which are being funded by respective States.

Achievements

The success of the first ETF raised for Dehradun was so encouraging that more such battalions were demanded by States and raised in subsequent years. In fact, this battalion has become a role model not only for Indian States but for countries the world over. As of 31 Dec 2010 figures, all ETFs put together, have planted and protected over 5.5 crore saplings in over 50,000 hectares of land. The following have been important highlights of these units:-

- Greening of Thar desert along Indira Gandhi Canal in Rajasthan.

- Rehabilitating the Mussorie mines in the Himalayas of Uttarakhand.

- Saving the Shivaliks from turning into a stone desert.

- Afforestation of difficult areas and restoration of forest wealth of Pithouragarh in Uttarakhand.

- Converting the vast barren land of Bhatti Mines in Delhi into a lush green area that is full of water bodies created painstakingly by ETF personnel.

- Creation of a lake in Amarpura area in Rajasthan ensuring a place for number of native and migratory birds.

- Conversion of Mohangarh area in Jaisalmer district of Rajasthan into lush green fields.

- Bringing awareness among natives of Assam about importance of forest cover and engaging them in participatory afforestation.

- Carrying out successful plantation in difficult areas of Shimla district and along banks and catchment areas of devastating Sutlej River in Himachal Pradesh.

- Ensuring stop to shifting ex-servicemen population to cities and towns in search of jobs by providing them second employment at their door steps.

In addition to above mentioned contributions made in the areas of their operations, ETFs have created state of the art nurseries, green houses, water ponds, vermiculture farms, check dams in mountain slopes and restored number of old water bodies.

INNOVATION AND INVENTION - AN INDIAN PERSPECTIVE

The Indian economic story over the last decade has clearly drawn the attention of the world, evidenced by the flood of heads of state who have visited India since 2010. Much of this traffic drew attention to India as a customer and consumer of foreign goods, a fact which was reflected in the big-ticket deals that India struck during the visits of the leaders of the US, Britain, France, Russia and China. The largest component of India's GDP is services, a statistic which lends itself to the question as to how much does or can India innovate or generate as intellectual property?

Some Indian companies are innovative in a limited sense in that they help localise the service to India, but these are not good working examples of innovation. The truly innovative technology companies in India are still struggling. The reasons boil down to two factors: lack of engineering talent and lack of commercial talent to scale businesses globally. The first is counterintuitive given the success of IIT graduates in California. India has good engineering schools, but it doesn't churn out enough of a class of engineers that think outside of the box. The second is a global issue - most of this talent is clustered in the Silicon Valley. But that will change over time.

The kind of activities being invested in and succeeding right now in India are businesses that either leverage inexpensive manpower (BPOs, agencies) or localize US successes. A frequent word used to describe domestic innovation in India is 'Jugaad'. The West calls this "reverse innovation", while some others call it "frugal" or "constraint-based" innovation."

Writing about the practice of frugal innovation in the New York

Times, David Bornstein chronicles the example of a Bihar company named Husk Power Systems, which has developed a technique to turn rice husk into electricity. According to Bornstein: " What the company illustrates is a different way to think about innovation — one that is suitable for global problems that stem from poor people's lack of access to energy, water, housing and education. In many cases, success in these challenges hinges less on big new ideas than on collections of small old ideas well integrated and executed."

Descriptions of innovation in India which originate in the frugal innovation paradigm speak primarily to innovation for India's domestic market, and not for global markets. By the same token, global companies like GE have research and development centres in India which produce intellectual property that is used globally. Despite successes by export-dependent industries in India, world perception clearly tilts toward that frugal innovation paradigm for India. While practical innovation or 'jugaad' in India may be lauded, and may even be termed as important for domestic markets, India's competitiveness as a global innovator lies in generating export-competitive innovation.

India's best chances to make its mark on innovation may be in cleantech and other disruptive technologies that can improve the quality of life for the world's poor while enriching their inventors and investors. One such invention along that vein, a low-cost, durable, prosthesis known as the Jaipur foot, has restored function to amputees the world over and is probably the best-known Indian innovation to have found a global market. Some other recent inventions that hold similar promise include the following:-

(a)   **Hybrid Electric and Kerosene Stove**. A hybrid electric/ kerosene stove that saves 70 percent on fuel costs compared with conventional stoves that burn liquefied petroleum gas. The stove uses a 6-V coil to heat kerosene for cooking. One litre of kerosene lasts for eight hours, and the stove consumes one unit of electrical power for every 20 hours of use.

(b)   **Mitti Cool**. Mitti Cool is the so-called village or rural fridge. Invented by a potter, Mitti Cool is made from special clay (mitti) and uses evaporation to cool three or more storage chambers for water, fruits and vegetables.

(c)   **Modified Lantern**.   A modified lantern produces light equal to a 100-watt bulb but runs on kerosene, diesel or ethanol. The lamp has a wick coated with high-temperature materials, such as silica; a self-cleaning nozzle; and a special glass that reduces the chances of explosion.

(d)   **Diesel Motorcycle cum Tractor**.   This is a diesel motorcycle that doubles as a tractor when the back wheel is removed and replaced with a spiked cylinder.

(e)   **Micro Windmill Charger**. This is a micro-windmill-based mobile charger that uses wind power to charge phones and laptops.

India was always a fertile land for innovations. The most notable Indian inventions range from number Zero to some high end technologies that we use every day. While many of these high-tech inventions are usually glorified, certain others which come from the 'soul of India'- villages are usually ignored. These inventions from the country's small corners cannot be designated as "life changing," but still they are powerful enough to propel the dreams of a small population and also motivate the generations to produce something good for the society.

India's rural innovators have proved that ordinary people are indeed capable of extraordinary inventions. Despite many constraints like lack of education and severe cash crunch, most of them have succeeded in using technology cost-effectively to build ingenious products. Regular exhibition of grassroots innovations is organised by the National Innovation Foundation (NIF), a grant-in-aid institute under the Department of Science and Technology (DST) set up in February 2000. The mission of NIF is to make India a global leader in sustainable technologies by building upon genius of grassroots technological innovators and traditional knowledge holders. The IGNITE is an annual competition organised by the NIF in association with Central Board of Secondary Education (CBSE), Society for Research and Initiatives in Sustainable Technologies and Institutions (SRISTI), various State Education Boards and other partners. In the competition, school students share their innovative ideas and offer solutions on local and global issues. Listed below are a few innovations which have changed the lives of a million Indians:-

(a)   **Washing cum Exercise Machine**. Remya, a high school girl from Kerala was forced to do laundry when her mother fell sick. Out of her dislike to wash clothes by hand, Remya invented a pedal-powered washing machine at the age of 14. The machine, which looks like the exer-cycle which we see in a gymnasium, consists of an aluminium cabin containing a horizontal cylinder made of iron net. The cylinder is connected to a pedalling system that consists of a cycle chain, pedals and a seat. Clothes are put in the cylinder, the cabin is filled with water and detergent is added and is left to soak for some time. Pedal it for three to four minutes after that and you are done! The cylinder rotates at a very high speed with the clothes inside, cleaning them thoroughly. The soap water drains out, the barrel is refilled and the process is repeated. By pedalling, the clothes also become about 80% dry. The Invention has many advantages. It doesn't require electricity to work, it is hugely affordable and moreover, it replaces your exercise machine.

(b)   **Water Walking Shoe**. This beautiful invention is from a village man of tremendous determination. His invention dates back to three decades. It is called the Water Walker, which comes handy in the flooded regions of India, even now. The shoes consist of two floats made of thermocol, bonded with a rexine sheet. This whole unit is attached to metal straps with back foot support. These two individual shoes are also tied to each other to prevent them from going apart beyond one's ability to steer them. The size of shoe gives good buoyancy and ease in manoeuvring. With a pair of hand held oars for balancing, a person can either walk or skate across the lake. Mr Chaurasia had demonstrated his shoes in front of the media at the Delhi Boat Club, which was widely covered. He was also interviewed by BBC at that time, which was great recognition for him. He had another invention on his name, "the amphibious cycle" which used the same principle of his shoes.

(c)   **Electric Painting Brush**.   Jahangir, a young student from the militancy hit Anantnag district of Jammu & Kashmir invented the electric painting brush, which is essentially a blessing to the painting workers. His invention avoids the need for dipping brush into the paint bucket, which decrease the tediousness of the job and saves paint. Jahangir was the son of a carpenter. He used to work while studying in order to help his poor family and also fund himself. One day he saw some workers painting a high wall near his house. They were struggling with the work as there is little space on the ladder to keep the paint bucket. They had to periodically dip the brush in the bucket and manage everything without losing the grip from ladder. The paint was also spilled over the worker's clothes. After seeing this, he was determined to reduce their effort. The automatic painting device he invented has a painting brush attached to a tube, which goes directly to a paint bucket via a motor which pumps the paint to brush. User can control flow of paint through a liver and the paint is equally distributed to bristles at 4 places through a distributor. His working prototype has great commercial potential along with wide usability.

(d)   **Tree Climbing Machine**. Late Mr MJ Joseph was an innovative farmer. After many of his innovations failed to gain popularity, including a fruit squeezer which could get juice out of any fruit, Joseph made the best invention of his life- a machine, using which anybody can climb a coconut or areca nut tree. Joseph made this machine under the guidance of his father. The climber consists of two metal loops with several sub-loops and connecting rods. There are two pedals, one right and one left, for placing the foot. The device is designed in such a way that once it is fastened to the tree using the attached ropes, you can use the pedal movements to climb. The cost effective, safe and convenient machine has become very popular in South India. Many modifications were made to the device and the National Innovation Foundation facilitated sale of this climber to customers in USA, Maldives, Thailand, Australia, Brazil and Mexico.

(e) **Cotton Harvester**. Mr Nattubhai Vader, a farmer from Gujarat invented the cotton harvester, a machine which can be fitted to a tractor for harvesting cotton. He was determined to make a machine for harvesting the troublesome variety of cotton, after he saw women and children performing the slow exhausting work in the fields. His determination paid off well as he designed and tweaked a massive apparatus of spinning rubber hoses and vacuums to fit over a tractor. The apparatus can pick as much cotton in one hour as 10 people can harvest in two days.

(f) **Well Pulley with a Brake**. In the villages, water is mainly drawn from wells. The traditionally designed pulley system is physically demanding, especially for the women folk. Realising the importance of pulley in the daily routine of average rural women, Mr Amit Agrawat decided to redesign it. He came up with a pulley attached to a braking system or a stopper. He made three pulleys- Ganga, Yamuna and Saraswati, which can be used according to the type of the well. The pulleys allow women to rest mid-way through their labour.

(g) **Water Tyres**. The village farmers of Madhya Pradesh were finding it difficult to work on the thick and hard soil in the fields with their tractors. It required them to put extra weight to the machine. The tractor salesmen were trying to sell them expensive weights to attach to vehicles. But the farmers invented an inexpensive and easy way by simply filling the tyres with water, which gave an added weight at literally, no cost. They not only saved money, but also invented something which benefitted millions of farmers across the country.

(h)   **Cotton Deseeder**. Mr Abdul Rahim Khan a farmer from the village of Mogra had many small inventions under his belt. Among that, his miniature cotton deeseeder is a miracle. It cost less than Rs 220 to make and saves 10 times as much each year in processing fees.

(i)   **Multipurpose Herbs Processor**. Mr Dharamveer was born as the 5th child of Ramswaroop Kamboj, who was a farmer and Savitri Devi who was an herbalist. He was attracted to the herbs at an early age, following his mother's passion. After seeking out different ways to lead his life, Dharamveer finally realised that agriculture is indeed the profession meant to him. Inspired from a bank manager, who promoted Aloe vera farming, Dharamveer started to cultivate it. But after realizing the huge cost of an Aloe vera gel extractor machine, he decided to build one on his own. After a number of prototypes, he was successful in building a table top machine capable of pulverizing and extracting oil or gel from various herbs including Amla and Aloe vera. The machine can cheaply make gel from the leaves and was widely recognised. Dharamveer give all the credit for his success to his mother, who instilled in him urge to know more about herbs.

(j)   **Reaper Windrower Machine**. Many times, in a standing crop, soybean pods shatter due to non-availability of labourers for harvesting the crop in time, leading to reduced yield and loss. To solve this problem Mr Bhagwan Singh decided to develop a reaper windrower machine. This device has three different units namely, cutting unit, which consists of cutter bar, reel unit for pushing the standing crop towards the cutter bar and gathering unit to windrow the crop at centre of the machine thus making it easy to handle/transport to the threshing floor. It reduces manpower requirement and the drudgery involved in the harvesting process. The machine has

7 ft width of operation and can cover 0.4 hectares per hour. While operating this machine, the fuel consumption of the tractor is around 2.5-3 litres per hour.

(k) **Hand Operated Water Pump**. Mr Sakthimainthan built a hand operated water pump in response to a dearth of available pumps that could be afforded by small farmers. He built five prototypes over a period of fifteen years before finally perfecting his design. The resulting water-lifting device is operated by the continuously rotating a handle. It is simple in design and has a high discharge at low cost compared to the motorised pumps and conventional hand pumps. The pump has discharge of 20,000 lph at 0.75 m head. The unit has also been tested by TNAU, Coimbatore and improved by CMERI Durgapur. It is useful device for drainage as well.

(l) **Bullock Operated Sprayer**. The bullock operated sprayer is pulled by a pair of bullocks and gets the drive from the ground through a gear box and belt pulley system. When the operator shifts the lever to a higher gear, the frequency of strokes of the pump increases as a result of which more pressure develops in the container. The spray fluid, thus, atomizes into fine droplets with a wider swath. This sprayer considerably reduces time requirement as compared to manual spraying and also the drudgery and health hazards involved in manual spraying. It has 18 nozzles, spaced at a distance of 35 cm and can cover 3.5 acre/hour.

(m) **Lime Cutter**. A small workshop owner from Uslampathy village in Tamilnadu, Mr M Nagarajan developed an innovative technology for cutting lime into small pieces in bulk quantity. This technology offers a great value proposition for the pickle manufacturing companies. The pickle industry suffers with a big problem of inefficiency in its operations due to low degree of automisation e.g. cutting of fruits is done manually. The second big problem, the industry faces is short-supply of labour during peak seasons, which limits the capacity. It is a novel machine in terms of its cost effectiveness, efficiency, drudgery reduction for women, safety considerations and transmission system.

(o)   **Automatic Thresher**.   As compared to other conventional threshers, Mr Ravi's thresher can be operated both automatically and manually with higher output and minimal damage. The Spices Board (Ministry of Commerce and Industry, Govt. of India) has recognised his innovation and included it in the Board's subsidy scheme. About 100 kg pepper can be threshed in a one HP machine in ten minutes (60 kg in a HP version). It consumes 3/4 electric units per hour, has threshing efficiency 90 per cent and the damage is about 2-3 per cent.

(p)   **Bio-waste Convertor**. Decomposed bio-waste has better fertility values as the decomposition can be fastened if the biomass is aerated, humidified and properly mixed. Mr Dhonshi's machine is a tractor driven machine, which can thoroughly mix the bio-wastes and add moisture as well thereby reducing the time of decomposition. The machine can cover a row of wastes disbursed by 100 trailers of size 11 ft x 6.5 ft x 2.5 ft (ie total 400 tonnes) in one hour. The tractor consumes 3.5-4.0 litre diesel per hour. The compost has better fertility value as compared to vermin compost. The total time for converting the biomass into manure while processed by this machine is 25-40 days, which is otherwise 3-4 months by conventional methods.

(q)   **Animal water Provider**. Lack of surface water sources and falling water table has made availability of clean drinking water a major problem in Rajasthan. For human beings, the need gets addressed to some extent but for animals this need is much less appreciated. Mr Swayambhoo Sharma came up with an interesting solution to address the drinking water needs of animals. He developed an arrangement such that every time people pump water for their use, 20 per cent of pumped water would directly go to fill an animal water trough. Since most people feel lazy in filling the drinking water trough for stray animals, this innovation solved the problem by a kind of tax at source. Another problem faced in hand pumps is that a single person finds it very difficult to pump and at the same drink water in the absence of a vessel for the same. Mr Chandan, then a first year student at IIM (A), came up with an idea of storing water in the body of the hand pump so that having pumped, one could use a tap and drink water like any other tap. Mr Yusuf Khan and Mr Madan Lal Kumawat, two other innovators, combined the ideas of Mr Chandan and Mr Swayambhoo Sharma and developed a hybrid model.

(r)   **Low Cost Milking Machine**.   Finding skilled labour for milking a small herd of cows is a problem faced by many farmers. But using machines for milking is a luxury which only a large farm or a dairy house can afford. Mr Raghava decided to develop some method of milking, which would be affordable for all farmers. The result was an easy to operate and low cost milking machine that could milk 1.5-2 litres of milk per minute. The machine can be used to remove all the milk from the udder. The cow feels as if it is being suckled and does not experience any pain.

(s)   **Shock Free Power Convertor**.   Mr Nicholson developed an innovative device which converts all electrical lines into shock-free power lines. This is a very useful device for every household as also for commercial establishments. The device can be installed just after the energy meter so that each and every connection in the building establishment gets connected to the device and becomes shock-free. The innovation has different variants based on application and user's requirements.

(t)   **Bamboo Stripper Machine**.   Bamboo needs to be stripped off its outer covering for developing a smooth surface to make interior decoration items and utility articles like cups, pen stands, etc. Doing the job manually is time consuming and laborious. The machine developed by Mr Toshi can do all the operations like removing the outer knots, smoothening the surface, internal/external carving and finishing. The machine has soft touch joystick controlled operating system, which facilitates precision in operation. The finished bamboo can be used to make bamboo pet bottles. This bottle has the potential to replace plastics and tin bottles and cans.

(u) **Mechanised Shuttle Loom**. This innovative mechanised shuttle loom simulates the working principles of traditional Manipuri shuttle loom, except that the new machine runs fully automatic with the help of a half-horse power motor. The output of the machine is 25-50 times more than the traditional shuttle loom and almost any other power loom. The innovative machine can weave 3-4 fabrics per hour in comparison to the traditional one which could barely make 1-2 fabrics in a day. Except for the change of bobbin, the machine doesn't require any manpower.

(v) **Double Shuttle Loom**. The innovative 'Double Shuttle Loom' works on the same principle as that of any other standard manual shuttle loom except that this new machine is broader in width and has a provision for two sets of warp rolls.

(w) **Contrast Weaving Loom**. The traditional Korvai or 'contrast' weaving involves intricate work where the design and the colour of the borders are often different from those of the main body of the sari. Three shuttles are needed: the weaver operates two, and an assistant operates the third. Ms Bhanumurti's automated system is derived from the "Catch Cord Technique drawing device for looms" so that no assistant is needed and the productivity is increased.

THE INDIAN FOOD REVOLUTION – A SUCCESS STORY

India has come a long way since independence when it was a low-income food-deficient country. Today the country is not only self-sufficient in rice and wheat, it also exports a range of food products and at any given time has up to 60 million tonnes of food grain buffer stocks. In a country as large as India it required visionaries like Mr MS Swaminathan, father of India's green revolution, and Mr BG Kurien, the father of India's white revolution to play a catalytic role in India's progress in the areas of crop and animal production and food security. These two revolutionary ideas of India have contributed greatly to the Indian success story.

From 130 million tonnes in 1980, India's food grain production has risen to over 245 million tonnes in 2012. With Operation Flood, milk production rose to 113 million tonnes from about 35 million tonnes in 1980, also making it one of the largest employers of rural people, especially women. Fish production has also grown substantially. Employing over 15 million people, India is now a major fish exporter. Development of water resources for irrigation has underpinned crop production. However, water scarcity and falling water tables have been a key concern in recent years. On the positive side, this has led to awareness that water is an exhaustible resource. As a result, the importance of judicious use of water is being increasingly recognised.

India has gone well beyond the realm of food production, covering issues like access to food and nutrition, livelihood, rural development and sustainable agriculture. With the looming impact of climate change and outbreaks of new strains of pests the requirements have become even more complex.

The White Revolution: Operation Flood

Operation Flood, a project of the National Dairy Development Board (NDDB) was the world's biggest dairy development programme which made India, a milk-deficient nation, the largest milk producer in the world, surpassing the USA in 1998, with about 17 percent of global output in 2011–12, which in 30 years doubled the milk available per person, and which made dairy farming India's largest self-sustainable rural employment generator. All this was achieved not merely by mass production, but by production by the masses.

The Anand pattern experiment at Amul, a single, cooperative dairy, was the engine behind the success of the programme. Mr Verghese Kurien was made the chairman of NDDB by the then Prime Minister of India,Shri Lal Bahadur Shastri, and he was the chairman and founder of Amul as well. Mr Kurien gave the necessary thrust using his professional management skills to the programme, and is recognised as its architect.

Operation Flood has created a national milk grid linking milk producers throughout India with consumers in over 700 towns and cities, reducing seasonal and regional price variations while ensuring that the producer gets a major share of the price consumers pay, by cutting out middlemen. By reducing malpractices, it has helped dairy farmers direct their own development, placing control of the resources they create, in their own hands.

The bedrock of Operation Flood has been village milk producers' co-operatives, which procure milk and provide inputs and services, making modern management and technology available to members. Operation Flood's objectives included an increase in milk production, akin to a flood of milk, to augment rural incomes and afford fair prices for consumers.

Operation Flood was implemented in three phases. Phase I (1970–1980) was financed by the sale of skimmed milk powder and butter oil donated by the European Union (then the European Economic Community (EEC)) through the World Food Programme.

NDDB planned the programme and negotiated the details of EEC assistance. During its first phase, Operation Flood linked 18 of India's premier milk sheds with consumers in India's major metropolitan cities: Delhi, Mumbai, Kolkata and Chennai, thus establishing mother dairies in four metros. Operation Flood Phase 1, originally meant to be completed in 1975, actually spanned the period of about nine years from 1970–79, at a total cost of Rs 116 crores. At the start of this operation in 1970 certain set of aims were kept in view for the implementation of the programmes. They included supply improvement by milk marketing in the organised dairy sector in the metropolitan cities of Mumbai, Kolkata, Chennai and Delhi. The objectives were to command a major share of the milk market and speed up development of dairy products in hinter lands of rural areas with a view to increase both production and procurement.

Operation Flood Phase II (1981–1985) increased the milk sheds from 18 to 136 and 290 urban markets expanded the outlets for milk. By the end of 1985, a self-sustaining system of 43,000 village cooperatives with 4,250,000 milk producers were covered. Domestic milk powder production increased from 22,000 tons in the pre-project year to 140,000 tons by 1989, with all of the increase coming from dairies set up under Operation Flood. The EEC gifts and World Bank loan helped promote self-reliance and direct marketing of milk by producers' cooperatives increased by several million litres a day.

Phase III (1985–1996) enabled dairy cooperatives to expand and strengthen the infrastructure required to procure and market increasing volumes of milk. Veterinary first-aid health care services, feed and artificial insemination services for cooperative members were extended, along with intensified member education. Operation Flood's Phase III consolidated India's dairy cooperative movement, adding 30,000 new dairy cooperatives to the 43,000 existing societies organized during Phase II. Milk-sheds peaked to 173 in 1988-89 with the number of women members and Women's Dairy Cooperative Societies increasing significantly. Phase III gave increased emphasis to research and development in animal health and animal nutrition. Innovations like vaccine for Theileriosis, bypassing protein feed and urea-molasses mineral blocks, all contributed to the enhanced productivity of milk producing animals.

The Green Revolution

India has quadrupled its food grain production since independence in 1947 and over the last three decades food grain production rose from 130 million tonnes to 240 million tonnes. Against this background of success, there have been periods when the rate of growth in food grain production gave cause for concern. Most recently this was in the period 1995-2005, when the growth in food grain output slumped. This was attributed to a decline in public spending and the Eleventh Five Year Plan helped correct this anomaly. However, food grain production is still strongly influenced by the annual monsoon and there are concerns on the likely negative impact of climate change. Given its current population growth rate, India will need to double its food grain production by 2050, which means growing another 5 million tonnes annually.

India's water resources, particularly in the context of agriculture, are facing extreme stress. The country sustains 16 percent of the world's human population and 20 percent livestock population with just 3 percent of the world's water. With changing lifestyles and rising water consumption in urban areas, water for agriculture is under threat from other users. Conflicts over access and control of water sources are becoming common, not only among people, but also among states within the country. Noting that by 2050, when India will need to double to its food grain production, conservation of water sources and judicious use of water will be the key to sustaining agricultural production in the coming years.

The Fisheries Sector

Over the last 30 years, there have been major changes in the scale and nature of the fisheries sector in India. From an industry based on small-scale artisanal production it now combines traditional techniques with a range of new technologies serving a vastly increased range of markets. India is the eighth largest fish producer in the world with an output of over 6.5 million tonnes per year. The share of inland fisheries has steadily increased, now comprising around 60 percent of total production. Much of this growth has come from the expanding aquaculture sector. Over 15 million people are engaged in the industry, with fishing serving as one among a series of livelihood strategies for small fishers. Fish and fish products have gained an important place in the export market, largely as a result of prawn farming that feeds export markets. Indian exports are estimated to comprise around 6 percent of the global trade in fish products, valued at over US $ 1.5 billion. India's 12th Five Year Plan lays stress on the importance of increasing sustainable production, particularly through improved deep-sea fishing and investing in inland fisheries.

Food Grain Buffers and Malnutrition

India today is the world's second fastest growing economy at 6% to 8% growth rate. It produces over 245 million tonnes of food grain annually of which 78% is wheat and rice alone. Our Public Distribution System (PDS) and ICDS, are the world's largest food subsidy programme. India procures 85 million tonnes food grains directly from the farmers for PDS, buffer and price stabilisation. Yet, for 63% population that depends on agriculture, the overall situation is bad. 253,000 farmers committed suicide during the period from 1995-2012, due to distress and debt. Millions of tonnes of food grain rot annually due to improper storage and maintenance and hence does not reach the poor, despite central food distribution programmes, employment as also social security programmes (Direct Food Support, Employment to Earn Food and Cash Assistance). 42.5% children are malnourished, more than 50% women are anaemic, 77% population survives on less than US 40 cents (Rs 20) per day and 80% do not get the prescribed level of energy (calories). There are 1.4 million child deaths every year and 65 million children are malnourished and a whopping 60 million stunted.

The question we need to seek an answer to is why is malnutrition endemic in India when the country is witnessing unprecedented progress, clocking the highest-ever growth rates since independence? Before seeking an answer to this question, here are a few more alarming statistics:-

(a)   An estimated 60 to 65 million people are displaced in India since independence, the highest number of people uprooted for development projects anywhere in the world.

(b)   Over 22 million people migrated from rural areas to urban areas over the past decade, the net migration share of rural-urban migration in urban growth increasing to 24 percent from 21 percent in the previous decade. For the first time since 1921, the urban population grew more than the rural population in the decade (increase of 91 million in urban vs 90.6 million in rural population) suggesting that distress migration may be a contributory factor propelled by a reduction in common property resources and livelihood means in rural areas.

(c)   As many as 225,000 farmers have committed suicide in despair at their economic plight during the last ten years alone.

(d)   During the current period of India's explosive growth and bumper harvests and seven million people for whom cultivation is the main livelihood quit farming in the decade covered by the 2011 census – averaging over 2,000 per day. This is a direct result of indebtedness to both financial institutions and moneylenders. The minimum support prices for different food grains announced by the government are usually below their actual production costs, rendering farming uneconomical. For example, the maximum selling price (MSP) for a quintal (100 kg) of wheat was Rs. 1,000 when the cost of production was Rs. 1,543.93 (Economic Survey 2011-12).

(e)   The government has consistently exceeded its

procurement target for food grains for the public distribution system (PDS) in recent years. The 75 million ton food grains purchased this year is several times more than its June 2012 target. There is a dearth of warehouses to store this grain and so around 25 million tonnes are kept in temporary open storage.

Food Grain Buffers and Food Rotting

Over the past four years, 5 million tonnes of food grain has rotted in open storage, leading the Supreme Court of India to make some caustic observations on the issue and urging the government to distribute the grain among the poor instead of letting it rot time and again. But the government, which terms malnutrition a 'national shame', told the court that the grain couldn't be distributed because of policy issues.

So what are the policies of the Indian state that lay the ground for such contradictions, forcing people to migrate, displacing them from their homes, compelling them to commit suicide, and denying them the right to food security and health while the country clocks 7 to 9 per cent growth rates? What are these policies that let food grain to rot but prevent the state from distributing it among the poor and starving?

An underlying pattern is evident, an economic and social dichotomy in Indian society that has been exacerbated by the neo-liberal reforms of the 1990s. It is a pattern in which precious natural resources are diverted at throwaway prices to the corporate sector, which is also given concessionary land and tax holidays in name of economic growth and development but cries itself hoarse at the 'wastage' of financial resources diverted to food subsidies for the poor and fertilizer subsidies for the farming sector. It is a pattern in which the state progressively abrogates its constitutional responsibilities to the people through privatization of its social welfare activities that exposes the poor to the supply-demand compulsions of market forces.

The popular media highlights this dichotomy as the two India's – India of the 'haves' and the other of the 'have-nots', one getting richer, and the other poorer.

In 1947, the people visualized the state playing the role of a guardian looking after the interests of the people. This idealistic belief saw the state progressively gaining ascendancy over the society and abrogating its responsibilities by fashioning policies to hand them over to other socio-economic structures. Society believed the state would be accountable and the people would remain its central concern, with the deprived sections receiving special attention and protection to ensure that inequality, exploitation and discrimination are eradicated.

Instead, modern concepts of development have seen the private sector, once protected by the state, emerging as such powerful force that, even the state finds difficult to control and rein in. The singular concern of state policy is to look for ways to achieve a higher growth rate, not to provide equal opportunity and access to the fruits of economic development. This approach has seen the emergence of a consumerist middle class that does not concern itself with the fact that the indulgences it enjoys cloak an insidious process of resource exploitation that is taking place on a national scale.

Behind this new middle class of the emerging capitalist order stands the forgotten class. It is a class that lives with the bitter everyday reality of wondering whether it will get work for the day and whether it will be able to meet its daily needs. It is a class that dreams at night that its young ones will sleep without starving and will get proper medical care when they fall ill.

Between its daily battles and nightly dreams lies a vast chasm. In India, that chasm is called development.

Food Bowl Overflowing

India today is sitting on one of the world's biggest hoards of food grains, about 66.7 million tonnes as of 01 January 2013. This is not some bizarre seasonal twist – monthly stocks of food grains averaged over 67 million tonnes for the whole of last year, including an all-time high of 80.2 million tonnes in June 2012. Just five years ago, in 2008, the food grains stock was 19.2 million tonnes on 01 January 208. Since then, it has zoomed up by almost 250 per cent to the present levels.

Government rules say that a buffer stock of 20 million tonnes and a strategic reserve of 50 million tonnes need to be maintained. But current stocks are more than two and a half times this benchmark.

This would be a matter of celebration except that even as food grain stocks keep piling up, hunger and malnutrition continue to haunt a quarter of the Indian population, over 200 million people, according to various estimates. Last year, India was ranked 65th in a list of 79 countries where serious hunger and malnutrition persists, made by the International Food Policy Research Institute. With over 43 per cent babies suffering malnutrition, on this count alone India is ranked below Ethiopia and Bangladesh. So how come a mountain of life-giving grain is surrounded by a sea of hungry humanity? The reasons can be found in a mix of subsidy cutting government policy, bureaucratic bumbling, corruption and even profiteering, say experts.

Successive bumper harvests since 2006, and better prices offered by the government procurement agencies have created these stocks. In April-March 2012, a record 380 lakh tons wheat was procured, while rice procurement during October 2011-September 2012, was also 350 lakh tons. This explains the huge stocks. But why can't it be distributed to the millions who need it? The government insists that it can only distribute food grain through its targeted public distribution system, fixed amounts, at low prices to those BPL, and at higher prices to those above the poverty line.

There are many problems with this approach, points out Biraj Patnaik, principal adviser to the Commissioners of the Supreme Court who is assisting the SC in tracking government policy. "The number of BPL families is based on projection for the year 2000 based on the 1991 Census. So their figures are off by 8-10 crore. We are trying to persuade them to adopt the 2011 population data," he says.

The committee headed by justice Wadhwa to suggest reforms in the public distribution system confirms this pointing out that the population of India was projected at 99 crore in 2000 whereas in 2012 it was 122 crore.

The poverty line itself is a matter of serious dispute because it is pegged at Rs 18 in urban areas and Rs 12 in rural areas per person per day. Many families that are technically above the poverty line are so poor that they can't afford the wheat and rice offered by the government at subsidised rates.

The most obvious solution is distribution to one and all. Economist Jean Dreze, a member of the NAC, sees the excess stock as a "great opportunity" to consolidate the Public Distribution System under the National Food Security Act. He said, "It could be used to facilitate the transition to a more inclusive if not universal PDS within a few years." The government, however, is not comfortable with this idea. And so, the warehouses will remain full in the months to come.

Supply Chain Management

The food sector in India is poised for rapid growth and structural transformation. The sector is already seeing substantial private and public investment with the objective of enhancing production, procurement, processing, distribution, and retailing efficiency.

In the years to come, the firms in the food sector will have to substantially improve their effectiveness and efficiency and meet increasingly high quality, consistency, and safety standards to comply with the stringent food laws and demands of export markets. These challenges will necessitate significant changes in the supply chain design and operation that gets the food from the 'land to mouth.' This will consequently raise new managerial challenges for meeting the specific demands for various users – processors, feed companies, exporters, retailers, and consumers. In addition, the players in the sector will have to address the policy and institutional concerns of integrating small farmers in modern value chains as well as streamlining traditional fragmented value chains to maximize share of consumer rupee going to the farmers.

A large part of the supply chain is in the semi-organised sector though aspiring to get more organized and professional. An integrated perspective of the supply chain with the objective of bringing professionalism and excellence in decision-making can significantly improve the effectiveness and efficiency of the supply chain and consequently the food business in India.

While supply chain management is a more generic concept applicable in all sectors - perishability, seasonality, variability, bulkiness, small-scale production, and traceability are some of the issues that distinguish the food supply chains. Similarly, while quality is again a generic issue, it is obviously more critical in the food supply chains. Finally, public policies and regulation have a significant role in influencing food supply chains since the 'product' is an essential good, every citizen is a consumer, and a significant percentage of the citizens are producers.

In the above context, managers in the food sector need to develop a wide and thorough supply chain perspective and, this programme, with a focus on building skills and knowledge required for meeting the challenges of modern and effective food supply chain management, will add significant value.

Annexure 10

PANCHAYTI RAJ

Background

Panchayats (a group of elected representatives of a village) have been the backbone of the Indian villages since the beginning of recorded history. In 1946, Gandhi Ji had aptly remarked that 'India's independence must begin at the bottom and every village ought to be a Republic or a Panchayat with powers.' Panchayat Raj is a system of governance in which 'Gram (Village) Panchayats are the basic units of administration. It has 3 levels: Gram (village, though it can comprise more than one village), Janpad (block) and Zilla (district). Raj literally means "governance or government". It is a decentralized form of Government, where each village is responsible for its own affairs. It is the foundation of India's political system. The passage of the Constitution (73rd Amendment) Act, 1992 (or simply the Panchayati Raj Act) marks a new era in the federal democratic set up of India. It provided the much needed constitutional sanction to the Panchayati Raj Institutions (PRIs) for functioning as an organic and integral part of the nation's democratic process. It came into force with effect from 24 April 1993. The salient features of the act are as enumerated. The act provided for the following provisions:-

(a) Constitutional status for Gram Sabha (village assembly).

(b) Three tier Panchayat system at the village, intermediate and district levels except in State with populations of less than 20 lakhs, where intermediate Panchayats may not be constituted,

(c) Reservation of seats and leadership positions for SCs/STs and women,

(d) Regular elections every 5 years,

(e) Establishment of independent State Election Commission,

(f) State Finance Commissions to be set up once in 5 years,

Powers, Authority and Responsibilities of Panchayats

The Constitution of India states "Powers to be so devolved upon Panchayats as to enable them to functions as institutions of self government (Article 243 G read with Schedule XI). Article 243 G reads "subject to the provisions of this Constitution, the Legislature of a State may, by law, endow the Panchayats with such powers and authority as may be necessary to enable them to function as institutions of self-government and such law may contain provisions for the devolution of powers and responsibilities upon Panchayats at the appropriate level, subject to such conditions as may be specified therein, with respect to:-

(a) Preparation of plans for economic development and social justice;

(b) Implementation of schemes for economic development and social justice as may be entrusted to them including those in relation to the matters listed in the Eleventh Schedule." The 11th schedule in the constitution lists 29 functional areas to be brought within the purview of the decentralized planning level, including agriculture and allied activities, irrigation, social forestry, village and small-scale industries, water supply, housing, roads, education and poverty alleviation programmes.

Thus, the Panchayats have been endowed with such powers and authority as may be necessary to function as institutions of self-government and social justice. Providing real functional autonomy at the village level is at the core of the concept.

Achievements

As a result of the enactment of the Act, 2,33,913 Village Panchayats, 26,56,476 elected representatives (37 % women, 19% SC and 12% ST), ST), 6094 Intermediate Panchayats, 1,56,609 elected representatives. (37 % women, 21 % SC, 7 % ST) and 537 District

Panchayats, 15,694 elected representatives. (37 % women, 17 % SC, 11 % ST) are functioning. This is the broadest representative base that exists in any country of the world – developed or under-developed.

Reservation for Women in PRIs in India

As per provisions of Article 243 D of the Constitution one third of the total number of seats to be filled by the direct election in Panchayats at all levels are reserved for women. A large number of States have legislated for 50% % reservation for women. As a result of this initiative out of 2.8 million elected members in Panchayats about a million are women. A recent survey has found that out of these Elected Women Representatives (EWRs):-

(a) Four-fifth of the EWRs did not have any one in their family in politics.

(b) 86% of EWRs are first timers.

(c) 14% were elected more than once.

(d) Sizable population of EWRs perceive enhancement in their self-esteem (79%), Confidence (81%) and decision making ability (74%) due to their participation in the Panchayat Raj institutions.

Powers and Responsibilities

Village-level Panchayats or Gram panchayats are local self-governments at the village level in India, and the Sarpanch (Head of Panchayat) is in charge of it. The gram panchayat is the foundation of the Panchayat System. A gram panchayat consists of between 7 and 17 members, elected from the wards of the village, and they are called "panch". People of village elect panchs. To establish a Gram panchayat in a village, the population of the village should be at least 750 people of voting age. The responsibilities of panchayat include agriculture and allied activities, irrigation, social forestry, village and small-scale industries, water supply, housing, roads, education and poverty alleviation programmes. In addition panchayats also perform the following functions:-

(a) Maintain street lights, construction and repair work of roads in villages and also hold the village markets, fairs, collection of tax, festivals and celebrations.

(b) Keep record of births, deaths and marriages in the village.

(c) Look after public health and hygiene by providing facilities for sanitation and drinking water.

(d) Providing free education.

Gram Sabhas

Gram Sabha includes all the adult citizen voters of the village. It is empowered to support or topple down the Gram Panchayat body. The Gram Sabha can contribute to a number of decisions taken by the Gram Panchayat and facilitate to modify the week decisions. Gram Sabhas have been given extensive powers to:-

(a) Safeguard and preserve traditions, customs, cultural identity community resources and customary mode of dispute resolution.

(b) Approve the plans, programmes and projects for social and economic development.

(c) Identify beneficiaries under poverty alleviation and other programmes, authorise the issue of utilization certificates after examining the utilisation of funds by the Gram Panchayat.

(d) Protect common property resources, including minor forest produce.

(e) Be consulted prior to land acquisition.

Block Panchayat

A Block Panchayat (panchayat samiti) is a local government body at the Development Block level. The samiti is elected for 5 years and is headed by the Chairman and the Deputy Chairman. The samiti is the link between the gram panchayat and the district administration. The Block Samiti is composed of ex-official members (all sarpanchas of the panchayats in the Block, the MPs and MLAs of the area and the SDO of the subdivision), co-opt members (representatives of SC/ST and women), associate members (a farmer of the area, a representative of the cooperative societies and one of the marketing services).

District Level Panchayat

The governing system at district level in Panchayat Raj is also popularly known as "Zilla Parishad". Chief of administration is an officer from the Indian Administrative Service (IAS) cadre. The District level Panchayat functions are as follows:-:

(a) Provide essential services and facilities to the rural population.

(b) Supply improved seeds to farmers. Inform them of new farming techniques.

(c) Set up and run schools and libraries in the rural areas.

(d) Start Primary Health Centres and hospitals in villages as also vaccination drives against epidemics

(e) Execute plans for the development of the scheduled castes and tribes. Set up free schools and hostels for them.

(f) Encourage entrepreneurs to start small-scale industries and implement rural employment schemes.

(g) Construct bridges, roads & other public facilities and their maintenance.

(h) Provide employment.

Conclusion

The concept of panchayats was a part of the philosophy of 'Purna

Swaraj' (complete self-governance) and 'Gram Swaraj"(village self-governance). Mahatma Gandhi and Jawaharlal Nehru breathed into those concepts an inexorable and practical patriotic impetus during the era of Indian struggle for independence. Indeed, at the seed time of our Constitution, the concept of village panchayats was not a remote and hoary historical concept. It was a part of the legacy of India's struggle for freedom and its quest for its own traditions and identity. Today it has become the broadest representative base that exists in any country of the world – developed or under-developed.

Annexure 11

MICRO, SMALL AND MEDIUM ENTERPRISES

Introduction

Micro, Small and Medium Enterprises (MSMEs), including khadi and village rural enterprises are credited with generating the highest rates of employment growth and account for a major share of industrial production and exports.   They also play a key role in the development of economies with their effective, efficient, flexible and innovative entrepreneurial spirit. The socio-economic policies adopted by India have laid stress on MSMEs as a means to improve the country's economic conditions.

Ministry of Micro, Small and Medium Enterprises designs MSME policies and promotes and facilitates programmes, projects and schemes and monitors their implementation with a view to assisting MSMEs and help them scale up.

Development and Promotion of MSMEs.

The primary responsibility of promotion and development of MSMEs is of the State Governments. However, the Government of India, supplements the efforts of the State Governments through various initiatives. The role of the Ministry of Micro Small and Medium Enterprises and its organizations is to assist the States in their efforts to encourage entrepreneurship, employment and livelihood opportunities and enhance the competitiveness of MSMEs in the changed economic scenario. The schemes and programmes undertaken by the Ministry and its organizations seek to facilitate/provide:-

(a) Adequate flow of credit from financial institutions/banks.

(b) Support for technology, up gradation and modernization.

(c) Integrated infrastructural facilities.

(d) Modern testing facilities and quality certification.

(e) Access to modern management practices.

(f) Entrepreneurship development and skill up gradation through appropriate training facilities.

(g) Support for product development, design intervention and packaging.

(h) Welfare of artisans and workers.

(j) Assistance for better access to domestic and export markets.

(k) Cluster-wise measures to promote capacity building and empowerment of the units.

The majorities of people living in rural areas draw their livelihood from agriculture and allied sectors. However, the growth and balanced development of other sectors such as industry and services is also necessary to sustain the growth of Indian economy in an inclusive manner. The Government of India is striving to improve the economic and social conditions of rural population and non-farm sector through a host of measures including creation of productive employment opportunities based on optimal use of local raw materials and skills as well as undertaking interventions aimed at improving supply chain; enhancing skills; upgrading technology; expanding markets and capacity building of the entrepreneurs/ artisans and their groups/ collectives.

Implementation of Policies and Programmes.

The implementation of policies and various programmes/ schemes for providing infrastructure and support services to MSME's is undertaken through its attached office, namely the Office of the Development Commissioner (MSME), National Small Industries Corporation (NSIC), Khadi and Village Industries Commission (KVIC); the Coir Board, and three training institutes viz., National

Institute for Micro, Small and Medium Enterprises (NI-MSME), Hyderabad, National Institute for Entrepreneurship and Small Business Development (NIESBUD), NOIDA, Indian Institute of Entrepreneurship (IIE), Guwahati and Mahatma Gandhi Institute for Rural Industrialization (MGIRI), Wardha.

The National Board for Micro, Small and Medium Enterprises (NBMSME) examines the factors affecting promotion and development of MSMEs, reviews existing policies and programmes and makes recommendations to the Government for formulating the policies and programmes for the growth of MSMEs.

The National Small Industries Corporation (NSIC) Ltd. NSIC was established in 1955 by the Government of India with a view to promote, aid and foster the growth of small industries in the country. NSIC continues to remain at the forefront of industrial development throughout the country with its various programmes and projects to assist the MSME in the country. The main functions of the Corporation are to promote aid and foster the growth of micro and small enterprises in the country, generally on a commercial basis. It provides a variety of support services to micro and small enterprises by catering to their different requirements in the areas of raw material procurement, product marketing, credit rating, acquisition of technologies and adoption of modern management practices, etc.

National Entrepreneurship Development Institutes. Entrepreneurship development and training is one of the key elements for the promotion of Micro, Small and Medium Enterprises (MSMEs), especially for creation of new enterprises by the first generation entrepreneurs. In order to inculcate the entrepreneurial culture amongst the first generation of entrepreneurs on a regular basis, the Ministry has set up three national level Entrepreneurship Development Institutes viz; National Institute for Micro, Small and Medium Enterprises (NI-MSME) (1960) at Hyderabad, National Institute for Entrepreneurship and Small Business Development (NIESBUD) (1983) at NOIDA (Uttar Pradesh) and Indian Institute of Entrepreneurship (IIE) (1993) at Guwahati, as autonomous societies.

These institutes are engaged in developing training modules; undertaking research and training; and providing consultancy services for entrepreneurship development and promotion of MSMEs, including enhancement of their competitiveness.

National Board for Micro, Small and Medium Enterprises (NBMSME). The development work in MSME's involves several Departments/ Ministries and several organisations of Central/ State Governments. To facilitate coordination and inter-institutional linkages, a National Board for Micro, Small & Medium Enterprises consisting of a total of 47 members has been constituted. It is an apex advisory body constituted to render advice to the Government on all issues pertaining to the MSME sector. The Minister in charge of MSME of the Government of India is the Chairman and the Board comprises among others State Industry Ministers, some Members of Parliament, Secretaries of various Departments of Government of India, financial institutions, public sector undertakings, industry associations and eminent experts in the field. The board meets periodically to take stock of the issues pertaining to the MSME sector.

Growth and Performance of Micro, Small and Medium Enterprises (MSMES)

The Micro, Small and Medium Enterprises (MSMEs) sector contributes significantly to the manufacturing output, employment and exports of the country. It is estimated that in terms of value, the sector accounts for about 45 per cent of the manufacturing output and 40 per cent of the total exports of the country. The sector is estimated to employ about 69 million persons in over 20 million enterprises throughout the country. Further, this sector has consistently registered a higher growth rate than the rest of the industrial sector. There are over 6000 products ranging from traditional to high-tech items, which are being manufactured by the MSMEs in India. The MSMEs provide good opportunities for both self-employment and wage employment.

MSME Technology Development Centres (MSME TDCs). MSME TDCs are product specific Centers to look into MSME's specific problems and render technical services, develop and upgrade technologies & manpower development and training in specific product groups like Foundry & Forging, Electronics, Fragrance and Flavour, Sport Shoes, Electrical MSME in areas with cluster of industries and some strategic areas, the Government of India have set up MSME- Testing Stations at Jaipur, Bhopal, Kolhapur, Hyderabad, Bangalore, Puducherry and Ettumanur. These Testing Stations extend facilities for testing of various products.

MSME-Development Institutes (MSME-DIs). MSME-DIs are providing techno managerial consultancy assistance and rendering necessary assistance to MSMEs by conducting various programmes like Seminars, Industrial Motivational Campaigns, Feasibility Reports, Area Survey Reports. They also provide Common Facility services.

Marketing Assistance and Technology Upgradation Scheme for MSMEs. The objective of this scheme is to enhance MSME's competitiveness in the National as well as International market through various activities such as Technology up gradation in packaging, skills up gradation/Development for Modern Marketing Techniques, Competition Studies of products, special components for North Eastern Region (NER), Identification of new markets through state/district level, local exhibitions/trade fairs, Corporate Governance Practices, Marketing Hubs and Reimbursement to ISO.

Design Clinics scheme for MSMEs. The main objective of this component is to bring the MSME sector and design expertise on a common platform and to provide expert advice and solutions on real time design problems, resulting in new product development, continuous improvement and value-addition for existing products. It also aims at value added cost effective solutions. The activities under the scheme are; organizing seminars, workshops in MSME clusters include design projects of MSME units. National Institute of Design (NID) Ahmedabad is working as nodal agency.

Promotion of Information & Communication Tools (ICT) in MSME Sector.

The main objective of the scheme is to encourage and assist the potential MSME clusters to adopt ICT tools and applications in their production & business processes, with a view to improve their productivity and competitiveness in national and international markets. The broad activity under this component includes identifying the potential MSME manufacturing clusters for ICT intervention, setting up of e-readinesss centre, developing web portals for cluster, skill development of MSME unit staff, preparation of local software solutions for MSME to enhance their competetitiveness, etc. and networking MSME cluster portals on the National Level Portals in order to outreach MSMEs into global markets. The scheme is being implemented in 100 clusters.

International Cooperation Scheme

Technology infusion and/or up gradation of Indian Micro, Small and Medium Enterprises (MSMEs), their modernisation and promotion of their exports are the principal objectives of assistance under the International Cooperation Scheme. The Scheme covers the following activities:-

(a) Deputation of MSME business delegations to other countries for   exploring new areas of technology infusion/ up gradation, facilitating joint   ventures, improving market of MSMEs products, foreign collaborations, etc.

(b) Participation by Indian MSMEs in international exhibitions, trade fairs   and buyer-seller meets in foreign countries as well as in India, in which   there   is   international participation.

(c) Holding international conferences and seminars on topics and themes of interest to the MSME.

India has signed MOUs with Indonesia, Mozambique, Korea, Botswana, Egypt, Cote d'Ivoire, Tunisia, Rumania, Rawanda, United

Maxican States, Uzbekistan, Lesotho, Sri Lanka, Algeria and Sudan.

Conclusion

Micro, Small and medium Enterprises (MSMEs) Sector has emerged as a highly vibrant and dynamic sector of the Indian economy over the last five decades. MSMEs not only play crucial role in providing large employment opportunities at comparatively lower capital cost than large industries but also helps in industrialization of rural and backward areas, thereby reducing regional imbalances, assuring more equitable distribution of national income and wealth. MSEMs are complementary to large industries as actual units and this sector contributes enormously to the socio-economic development of the country.

CIVILIAN CAPACITY BUILDING : THE SPIRITUAL DIMENSION

'We are not human beings having a spiritual experience; we are spiritual beings having a human experience'

–Pierre Teilhard de Chardin.

We customarily measure the cost of any conflict/violence or disaster, natural or otherwise, in terms of money, lost production and number of civilians, soldiers and/or militants killed. But the most painful and costly legacy of conflict of any kind is the individual human suffering – the emotional/spiritual breakdown! Do we realize that the psychological wounds are worse than physical ones? We read about combatants returning from war zone being traumatized but what about the trauma and the psychological stress faced by the civilians who continue to live in the war ravaged zones?

Psychological support has to be given to people to rehabilitate them in the true sense. Just as Phoenix rises from its own ashes, they have to rise to fresh challenges of life again from the depth of hopelessness created by the trauma of violence / conflict / disaster. A simple and practical program is needed, besides other aids, to assist people to get back their self-esteem, dignity and faith in themselves. Yes, we need to factor in the spiritual dimension to the civilian capacity building that we talk of. Spirituality is the intangible dimension of peace building.

From experience I know peace cannot be achieved by force of discipline, by rules, regulations or by forcibly maintaining law and order in any region. For peace building we must find a new path, a path that does not impinge on any one's freedom, true or imagined.

Diversity of religion, ethnicity, and many cultural aspects hold people against each other creating a barrier to achieving harmony.

Keeping the above in mind, one of the best possible ways for peace building and sustaining it is through spiritual science.

Before saying anything further about spirituality I want to point out the difference between religion and spirituality. Spirituality is distinct from religion. Religion, unlike spirituality, can be potentially divisive in certain circumstances. "Religion is a human invention that centers on specific rituals and a set of stories that outline a basic moral code and belief system, while, spirituality relates to the spirit or essential essence of humanity. People, who say they are spiritual, are working to grow and better this inner force" says the website www.differencebetween.net. "Spirituality is a concept of an ultimate immaterial reality. It is an inner path enabling a person to discover the essence of his/her being "says www.wikipedia.org. Actually, spirituality cannot be clearly defined. The moment we try to define a thing, we limit it, and spirituality cannot be limited as it is a path to the boundless awareness which is way beyond our conscious mind's comprehension. The only way to know it is to experience it!

How Spirituality Works and What to Expect by the Practice of Spiritual Techniques

Practice of spirituality brings a shift in our consciousness. We can say spiritual science bridges the known and the unknown worlds. It works both in physical and non-physical states to bring peace, harmony etc. in our awareness. A spiritual approach facilitates outer change through individual empowerment. Spirituality enhances human values such as compassion, empathy, non-violence and tolerance. The practice of spirituality makes us realize that we are much more than mere helpless human body and mind. This realization gives us freedom from limitations and leads us to our inherent peace and confidence in ourselves, in spite of any outer circumstances. This training in spiritual practice will not only bring peace at the present moment, but it will slowly but surely lead to future peace in the region as well. When we, the individual, are at peace, peace will reign in the whole region! It is said that the practice of spiritual technique adds a powerful, much needed dimension of healing whenever human limits are reached. The spiritual approach fosters a positive attitude even in the most heart-rending situations.

We can take the example of Yogic spiritual tradition which provides tools such as Yoga, meditation and mindfulness. Practice of these tools brings an inner change in our consciousness leading to compassion, non-violence, empathy, tolerance and love of peace. According to W.H.O, patients and physicians have begun to realize the value of spiritual elements such as compassion, hope, peace etc. in every healing process.

To start a spiritual practice in the aftermath of conflict/war, small groups of local people/volunteers can be trained by us, who, later on, can train/teach other local people in the region to bring lasting peace.

Who Can Benefit From Spiritual Practice

The truth is – everyone can benefit from the practice of spirituality. It is non-discriminatory and does not even differentiate between good and bad. Actually there is no duality in spiritual science! It helps every section of society, from militants, dictators and estranged youth to victims, prisoners and security forces, transforming hate and bitterness to a balanced and a peaceful attitude. It is not limited to any one religion or culture.

Children traumatized and youth confused by the violence of conflict/war will greatly benefit by spiritual practices. It holds good for the perpetrators of violence too. If they practice spirituality their views will change and they, sooner or later, will have a fair and a balanced attitude.

When Can it be Used for Best Results

Best time to use spiritual practice is when a conflict of any kind is brewing. It will be most profitable for the whole region if the leaders and policy makers practice it as it always brings clarity of thought. It should be taught to the troops/soldiers before they are deployed and sent to difficult and hostile regions. It will be very useful in rehabilitation work of all kind, psycho-social recovery, trauma counseling/therapy, empowerment of women, building educational infrastructure, re-integrating former combatants into civilian society, building bridges between different communities, achieving sustainable peace, preventing conflict from restarting, rehabilitating prisoners, refugee camps, disaster relief, empowerment of children exposed to abuse and violence and educating youth. Exposure to violence of conflict/war makes youth both victims and perpetrators of that violence.

Some Examples

Cambodia suffered tremendous destruction under Khmer Rouge regime including the massacre of an estimated 1.7 million people between 1975 and 1979. In 1992, the first peacewalk Dhammayietra was initiated to promote the spiritual ideal of Buddhism- compassion, loving kindness, honesty and tolerance. This has given a sense of peace to the people after years of terrible violence.

David Steele, senior reconciliation facilitator, The United States Institute of Peace's Baghdad office in Iraq has conducted more than 35 conflict resolution Seminars for religious groups in various parts of the former Yugoslavia. According to David Steele, one of the most important elements in reconciliation process in the aftermath of violence and conflict is the feeling of empathy. Empathetic listening is essential for conflicting groups to be humanized and for the people to go beyond the feeling of victimization and to feel forgiveness for the "other". Empathy and forgiveness are basic qualities of spirituality.

"Art of Living" is an international, non-profit, educational and humanitarian organization founded by spiritual teacher Sri Sri Ravishankar. Since 2003 more than 5000 people from Baghdad, Basra, Suleymania and Karbala participated in The Art of Living Trauma Relief program. In 2006, inspired by the program's benefit, 43 people from these regions volunteered to become program instructors. There are now 50 A.O.L. instructors and150 registered volunteers in that country.

"There is anger and hatred all round Iraq. Iraqis need to learn how to manage anger and reconcile with the present. This requires a shift in the mind and a change of heart. That is where spirituality has a big Role to play" – says Sri Sri Ravishankar, spiritual leader.

In 2007 Prime Minister of Iraq Nouri Al-Malki emphasized that the Art of Living Foundation had played a key role in rebuilding Iraq. He said, "There are big powers which have big might, but they are not able to unite the hearts and minds of people. This work can be done only by spiritual leader".

Some Testimonials

"I actually use to look forward to fights. But now, since doing this course, I am totally different person. I can now walk away from a fight" –Inmate, Pollsmoor Prison, Cape Town, South Africa. "I suggest that such training programs be implemented for troops in all war affected regions." -G.M.Kolmikov, Ministry of Domestic Affairs, Russia. "I never realized I could get so high on breathing. Wow. I feel so relaxed and peaceful and I have done it just on my own breath" – Minor Challenger Memorial Youth Centre, Los Angeles, USA.

We are interested in building new peaceful relationships between the warring communities/states/countries. Developing some form of spiritual awareness is absolutely essential for bringing about this shift in consciousness. Spiritual practice initiates and sustains this shift towards peace. Spirituality, apparently intangible, is the most important component of peace building process. It has, so far, never been given the importance that is due to it, especially in psycho-social recovery process, maybe because it gets mixed up with religion.

It is time that spirituality was brought in the main stream of peace building process. Having knowledge of spirituality is a privilege, a privilege we need to use for the benefit of future generations. For a peaceful tomorrow we have to incorporate spiritual practice in peace building process TODAY! Be the alchemist! Transform the peace building process by including spiritual dimension to it!

Annexure 13

CLUSTERS and LEAD AGENCIES

Clusters and Sub Clusters	Lead Agency	Resource Centres	Agencies to Maintain Roster	Remarks
SAFETY and SECURITY				
(a) Community Violence reduction	MHA	Police and CRPF	MHA, DG CRPF and PMF	Retired officers can be rostered as experts
(b) Disarmament, Demobilisation and Reintegration	-do-	Police and PMF	-do-	-do-
(c) Mine Action	MHA and MOD	Army, Police, PMF and Pvt companies	MHA, PMF, DGR	-do-
(d) Police	MHA	Police, CRPF, PMF	-do-	-do-
(e) Protection Of Civilians	MHA	Police, State Governments, NGOs	DGs Police, PMF and State Govt	
(f) Security Sector Reforms	MHA and MOD	Police, BSF, Army	DGs Police, BSF, DGR	-do-
JUSTICE				
(a) Prison Correction Reforms	MHA	DG Prisons	MHA	-do-

(b) Judicial and Legal System Reforms	Min of Law and Justice	Bar Association, Bar Council of India, Consultancy Development Centre	Bar Association of India and Min of Law and Justice Consultancy Development Centre	Retired Judges and Constitutional experts can be identified and Roster
INCLUSIVE POLITICAL PROCESS				
(a) Constitutional Process	Min of Law and Justice	Bar Association, Bar Council of India, Consultancy Development Centre	Min of Law and Justice Bar Association of India Consultancy Development Centre	Experts on Constitution can be Rostered
(b) Elections and Electoral Process	Election Commission of India (EC)	ESI and MHA	MHA and ECI	Election Experts can be rostered
(c) Mediation, good offices and Conflict Resolution	MHA	MHA and Consultancy Development Centre (CDC)	MHA and CDC	
HUMANITARIAN COORD				
(a) Agriculture	Min Of Agriculture	Min of Agriculture, Min of Agro and Rural Industry, Agricultural Universities and Institutes.	Min of Agriculture and Min of Agro and Rural Development.	

(b) Education	Min of Human Resource Development	Min of HRD and Universities MHA(DOPT), CDC	Min of HRD CDC
(c) Health	Min of Health and Family Welfare	Min Of Health, Medical Colleges, Pvt Hospitals and Medical Council of India	Medical Council and CDC
CORE GOVT FUNCTIONALITY	MHA	MHA	
ECONOMIC REVITALIZATION			
(a) Employment Generation	Min of Labour and Employment	Min of Lab and Emp and Dte Gen of Employment and Training, ITI and ITCS	Ministry Labour and Employment Dte Gen of Trg and CTC
(b) Rural Employment	Min of Rural Development	Min of Rural Development Min of Agro and Rural Industry	Min of Rural Development and Min of Agro Rural Industry
(c) Private Sector and Industrial Development	Min of Commerce and Industry	Ministry of Commerce and Industry, Min of Micro, Small and Medium enterprises	Ministry of Commerce and Industry, Min of Micro, Small and Medium Enterprises

MINISTRY OF EXTERNAL AFFAIRS (MEA)

DPA (SINGLE POINT CONTACT FOR INTERNATIONAL AGENCIES)

MINISTRY OF HOME AFFAIRS (MHA)

NODAL MINISTRY FOR CIV CAP

CLUSTERS

	SAFETY AND SECURITY		JUSTICE		POLITICAL PROCESS		HUMANATARIAN COORDINATION		CORE GOVERNMENT FUNCTIONALITY		ECONOMIC REVITALISATION	
	SUB CLUSTER	LEAD AGENCY	SUB CLUSTER	LEAD AGENCY	SUB CLUSTER	LEAD AGENCY	SUB CLUSTER	LEAD AGENCY	SUB CLUSTER	LEAD AGENCY	SUB CLUSTER	LEAD AGENCY
	VIOLENCE RE-DUCTION	MHA	PRISON	MHA	CONSTI-TUTION	MIN OF LAW & JUSTICE	AGRICUL-TURE	MIN AGRICUL-TURE	GOVT FUNC-TIONAL-ITY	MHA	EMPLOY-MENT GENERA-TION	LABOUR & EMPLOYMENT

		JUDICIAL REFORMS	MIN OF LAW & JUSTICE	ELEC-TION	ECI	EDUCA-TION	HRD			RURAL EM / RURAL DEVEL-OPMENT	PLOY-MENT
				CON-FLICT RESOLU-TION	MHA	HEALTH	HEALTH & FAMILY WELFARE			MIN OF COM-MERCE & INDUSTRY	INDUS-TRIAL DEVELOP-MENT
DDR	MHA										
MINE ACTION	MHA										
POLICE	MHA										
PROTECTION CIVILIANS	MHA										
SSR	MHA & MOD										

BIBLIOGRAPHY – CIVCAP PROJECT

Expanding the Civilian Role in Peace Operations: Assessing Progress and Addressing Gaps, Workshop Summary of Experts Workshop: South America, Rio de Janiero, Brazil, April 2011.

Staff Support Unit for Capacity Building Activities of Jawaharlal Nehru National Urban Renewal Mission and other Schemes of the Ministry of Urban Development. Annual Report, Government of India, Ministry of Urban Development, 17 May 2012.

Report of Workshop on Assessment Methods for Roster Candidates, Berlin, 17 and 18 May 2012, Centre of International Peace Operations.

Addressing the Civilian Peace Keeping Capacity Gap, Cedric de Conning, Conflict Trends.

Civilian Roles in Peace Operations, Sharon Wiharta and Stephanie Blair, SIPRI Yearbook 2010: Armaments, Disarmament and International Security, pp 87-147.

Annual Report 2011-12, Ministry of Personnel, Public Grievances and Pensions, Government of India.

Strengthening Human Capital Through Capacity Building and Training, Dr Jaya S Anand, Institute of Management in Government, Thiruvananthapuram, India.

The Evolution of Regional Actors' Peace Building Capacity: The European Union and its Twin Track Approach to Peace Building in Macedonia, Mejlina Modanu, The North-South Institute, Ottawa, Canada.

Strategic Plan of Ministry of Urban Development 201-2016, Ministry of Urban Development, Government of India.

Justice Rapid Response – Lessons Learnt from Training Rostering and Multilateral Deployment of Civilian Experts, Justice Rapid Response Secretariat, New York.

A New Start for EU Peacemaking: Past Record and Future Potential, Emma Johansson et al, UCDP Paper No 7, Department of Peace and Conflict Research, Uppsala University, Sweden.

The Evolution of Organizational Learning in the UN Peace Operations Bureaucracy, Thorsten Benner et al, Learning to Build Peace? United Nations Peace Operations and Organisational Learning, Global Public Policy Institute, Berlin, June 2011.

New Players Through Old Lenses, Why History Matters in Engaging With Southern Actors, Eleanor Davey, HPG Brief No 48, Humanitarian Policy Group, July 2012.

Report of the Panel on United Nations Peace Operations, United Nations General Assembly Security Council, A/55/305–S/2000/809 of 21 August 2000.

The Brahimi Report: Four Years On, Proceedings of Workshop held at Geneva Centre for Security Policy, 20-21 June 2004, Thierry Tardy.

Built on Shaky Groung: A comprehensive Approach in Practice, Philipp Rotmann, Research Paper No 63, NATO Defence College, Rome, December 2010.

Brainstorming Report on Towards the Development of a Framework Methodology for Training Delivery in Civilian Crisis Management, E Barago et al, Berlin, 08-09 November 2010.

Protection of Civilians in Peacekeeping in Africa, Conflict Trends, Issue No 2, ACCORD.

Statement by Ambassador Manjeev Singh Puri, Deputy Permanent Representative of India at the United Nations, at The Special

Committee on Peace Keeping Operations on 23 February 2011.

Statement by Ambassador Manjeev Singh Puri, Deputy Permanent Representative of India at the United Nations on Post Conflict Peace Building at The General Assembly Plenary on 19 March 2012.

Statement by Ambassador Manjeev Singh Puri, Deputy Permanent Representative of India at the United Nations, in the Security Council Debate on SAG's Report to SG on Civilian Capacity Review on 12 May 2011.

Statement by Ambassador Hardeep Singh Puri, Permanent Representative of India at the United Nations on Briefing on UN Office of Central Africa/ Lords Resistance Army at The UN Security Council on 14 November 2011.

Statement by Ambassador Hardeep Singh Puri, Permanent Representative of India at the United Nations on Open Debate on Impact of Transnational Crime on Peace Security and Stability in West Africa and the Sahel Region at The UN Security Council on 21 February 2012.

Statement by Ambassador Hardeep Singh Puri, Permanent Representative of India at the United Nations on Debate on UNAMA at The UN Security Council on 20 March 2012.

Review of International Humanitarian Rosters by GHK Consulting Limited to the Ministry of Foreign Affairs of Denmark on 04 October 2010.

A New Partnership Agenda; Charting a New Horizon for Peace Keeping, Department of Peacekeeping Operations and Department of Field Support, New York 2009.

Adapting Norwegian Civilian Capacity for the Future: Implications of the Guéhenno Report, John Karlsrud, NOREF Policy Brief No 5, September 2011, NUPI.

Peace Building Review, October 2010, United Nations Peace Building

Support Office, New York.

Peacekeeping Training Centres in Africa, Middle East and Asia, Centre for International Peace Operations, Berlin.

Recovering From War: Gaps in Early Action, Rahul Chandran et al, Report by the NYU Centre on International Cooperation for the UK Department for International Development, New York, 01 July 2008.

Report Workshop on Management of Rosters for Deployable Civilian Capacity, CivCap 03/2010,

Report on the Strengthening of the United Nations System, United Nations General Assembly Security Council, A/65/747–S/2011/85 of 22 February 2011.

Report of the Secretary-General on Peace Building in the Immediate Aftermath of Conflict, United Nations General Assembly Security Council, A/63/881–S/2009/304 of 11 June 2009.

For the Honour of India, A History of Indian Peacekeeping, Lieutenant General Satish Nambiar, PVSM, AVSM, VrC (Retd), Centre for Armed Forces Historical Research, United Service Institute of India.

Report of the Secretary-General on Civilian Capacity Building in the Aftermath of Conflict, United Nations General Assembly Security Council, A/67/312–S/2012/645 of 15 August 2012.

About The Editors

Lieutenant General PK Singh, PVSM, AVSM (Retd)

Lt General PK Singh is the Director of the United Service Institution of India, New Delhi since 1st January 2009. During his military career spanning 41 years he participated in active counter-insurgency operations and the Indo-Pakistan War of 1971. He retired from active service in September 2008 as C-in-C (Army Commander). His academic qualifications include M Sc, M Phil and a Post Graduate Diploma in Business Management. He is a Council Member of the Indian Council of World Affairs, and Advisor to the Fair Observer, USA.

Brig V K Saxena

Brigadier V K Saxena (retd) was commissioned in Infantry and has served in the Indian Army for 35 years. During his military career he has served in various Command and Staff appointments. He has participated in active counter-insurgency operations and has served as Deputy Director General, Army Liaison Cell at the Army Headquarters. Post retirement he has served as Media Consultant in the Home Department of Government of Jammu & Kashmir.

Capt Sandeep Dewan, IN

Sandeep Dewan, a Master of Philosophy in Defence and Strategic Studies, is presently a Research Fellow at the Centre for Strategic Studies and Simulation at the United Service Institution of India, New Delhi. His fields of interest are Indo China relations, the Tibet dispute and matters maritime.

He has published articles and papers on Maritime Domain Awareness, PLA Navy, Asia Pacific security issues and piracy in the

Indian Ocean. He has presented papers on "India and the Asia Pacific Sea Lanes" at the 3rd Xiangshan Forum at Beijing and on "China's Quest for Seas Beyond its Shores" at the National Security Seminar at USI. He has also published papers in and has been a member coordinator of several projects undertaken by the USI namely, "Strategic Directions China", "India's Comprehensive National Power A Place in the World" and "Civilian Capacity in a Changing World Order".